Break Through
Featuring
Raison Thompson

Break Through
Featuring
Raison Thompson

Powerful Stories
from Global Authorities
That Are Guaranteed
to Equip Anyone for
Real Life Breakthrough

Raison Thompson
Johnny Wimbrey
Nik Halik
Les Brown
and other leading authorities

WIMBREY TRAINING SYSTEMS
SOUTHLAKE, TEXAS

ISBN: 978-1-951502-25-6

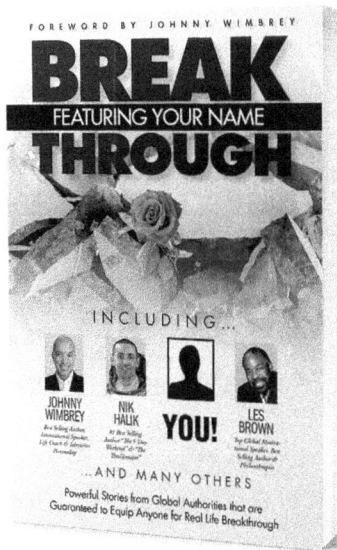

TABLE OF CONTENTS

Foreword

Think back to the hardest, darkest times in your life. What were you going through? How many times did you fail? How did you break through the difficulties and barriers you faced? How did you finally reach the success you knew you deserved?

Why do I ask this? Why do I care about the bad times and failures in your life? I care because how you handled the bad times tell me what type of person you are. I care because the choices you make when you face failure and the lessons you learn as you break through define you.

I can feel your skepticism. You think, really? Failure's important? Why?

Well, I know this to be true. I have had failures and troubles, and my choices turned me into the man I am today. I managed to break past and break through those times.

This is true, too, with the amazing group of authors I have asked to join me in *Break Through*.

I am honored to be joined by the men and women who have made deliberate sacrifices to contribute chapters to this book. Les Brown, Nik Halik, and every one of our other authors will inspire you with their stories of how they broke through their failures and barriers.

All had pain, rejection, and setbacks, and all were able to assess where they were and to make the necessary choices. Every author honestly shares their mistakes and successes with us.

Our *Break Through* authors are brave and fascinating, full of faith in their futures, and generous with their truths. They will help you navigate the crossroads you encounter and help you make sure your choices send you down the path of empowerment, confidence, and success. I am confident they will help you on your journey.

I introduce you now to my *Break Through* partners. Each one is someone I am proud to call a co-author and friend.

—**Johnny Wimbrey**

CHAPTER ONE

Inspect
What You Expect

Johnny Wimbrey

There are many things upon which I am not an authority, and there are many areas in which I will never be able to claim to be an expert, but I can tell you with total confidence that I *am* the authority on the expectation of success.

Every day, I wake up with the expectation for another level of success. I *expect* to find success mentally, emotionally, spiritually, financially, with love, with compassion, and with sensitivity.

I know I will have more of everything that matters to me, and it's just not material things. I crave and expect more knowledge, more honesty, and more good people in my life. My expectation is not arrogant, it's not greedy. My expectation is an intrinsic part of me, and I have honed it and practiced it since I was eighteen years old.

I am Johnny Wimbrey. I am a public speaker and entrepreneur, known around the world for inspiring people and helping them to change their lives. I have built a wonderful life with my wife and children. Now I'm in the privileged position of being able to give back to my community and around the globe.

No one, myself included, would have expected this—let alone predicted it—based on who I used to be. The choices I made, however, made me the man I am today.

Rejection framed my young life. My earliest memory is being hungry in a shelter for battered women. I was three years old and wanted some milk that I found when I opened the refrigerator door. Someone slammed the door on my fingers and told me the refrigerator wasn't ours and the milk wasn't mine to drink because it belonged to another family at the shelter.

That was probably the moment I grasped the unhappy facts: Yes, my mother had left my abusive, alcoholic father; we were temporary guests in a battered women's shelter; my two older brothers and I were homeless.

That feeling of rejection became the mainstay of my childhood and adolescence. My brothers, mother, and I had fled from Texas to California and I didn't see my father for years. I thought he rejected us.

My mother sent us back to live with him a few years later, and I didn't see her for the next three years of my life. More rejection. It was better to think she was dead than she had rejected us. I spent my elementary school years with my unpredictable, alcoholic father who was always busy, doing my best to keep up with my two big brothers: one a future felon, the other a future minister.

I didn't ask to move to California; I didn't ask to be sent back away from my mother, I definitely didn't ask to live with my father again. Looking back, though, I'm so glad I did live with him during those formative years. He gave me the basis for my understanding of expectation.

My father worked as a trash collector for the city. He didn't work in our poor neighborhood; his route took him over to the other side of town, the *rich* side of town. Every year when we had the long Christmas school holiday, my dad took us three boys along after work.

My father wanted us to see what else was out there in the world. He wanted us to see all the things we could have. He pushed us to open our eyes to the innumerable possibilities we had in front of us. Those trips taught me to despise the word *average*. My father raised my expectations. Not then, but later in my adolescence, I took it upon myself to rise to the challenge.

My own expectation for daily increase comes from a garbage man who refused to allow me to accept "average." He taught me to train my vision.

It took me a while to perfect this vision. It was focused on the wrong things in high school, when I made some of the worse decisions of my life. Unfortunately, my focus involved cigarettes, alcohol, drugs, and guns. My teachers told me they saw potential and talent in me and I ignored them. Who were they to tell me how to run my life? I was barreling down a one-way path headed to gang violence, substance abuse, prison, and a literal dead end.

When I was eighteen years old and a junior in high school, my path took a sudden turn when my good friend Mookie was killed by a rival. I went to Mookie's wake to say goodbye, and my brain was teeming with thoughts of death, grief, anger, and vengeance. I packed my gun as I got dressed that evening. I was looking for revenge, ready for a fight, with no glimmer of consequences or the future in my thoughts.

Brooding in my pew, I was barely listening to the speakers until Mookie's mother got up. I knew her, so I gave her the courtesy of listening to her fully. She talked with grace about my dear friend, her son, expressing not only her pain for his loss but actual forgiveness. She stood in front of Mookie's friends, family, and community and forgave her son's murderer. There was no room for interpretation:

"I forgive the man who shot my son."

She could have easily given in to her own anger and thoughts of revenge. She could have lashed out at those who loved her or withdrawn from her life altogether. But she didn't. If Mookie's *own mother*, the woman who loved him more than anyone else on this earth did, could forgive, what right did *I* have to seek vengeance?

A switch went on in my brain. I *knew* this moment was going to change my life. I knew my sudden awareness came straight from God. I was sitting there, conscious and aware, and I heard it clearly, just as if He had leaned over and whispered it directly into my ear: *This will change your life.*

I didn't hear Him because I was better or smarter than everyone around me; I was just ready to listen. God's message was flowing over everyone who was sitting with me; I was tuned to "receive."

I leaned forward and looked up and down the pew. My friends were radiating energy and anger. I could almost see the waves of vengeance coming off their bodies. Two seconds earlier, I was just like them. No more. The moment I changed, sitting there in the pew at Mookie's wake, I knew I expected more than I had the moment before.

My body stilled and I started breathing deeply. If I could have seen into the future, I would have known that every one of Mookie's and my friends would get long-term prison sentences. Perhaps I already did know this.

I knew we had been headed down the same path to the

same dead end. I knew I could have more than this. *I could be more than this.*

After everyone said their "peace" and we were milling around outside, I pulled Reverend Fitzgerald aside.

"Can I talk to you for a second?"

"Of course, son. What is it?"

"I want to give you my gun. If I give you my gun, I know I won't do anything crazy. Reverend, please take it. I don't want to live like this anymore. I am serious this time."

"You know if you give this to me, I'm not going to give it back."

"Yes, sir."

That was it. I gave him my gun. I stopped selling drugs. I stopped breaking the law. I just stopped. The next day I met Crystal, who became my wife a few years later.

I walked away from the life I had been leading. I said I was changing. And I did.

I was blessed with the chance to take what I had been given and use it to climb up and out. My prayers, my conversations with God, and the knowledge that He would give me what I needed when I needed it most, helped me every step of the way. My accomplishments didn't just belong to me; I knew I was being watched and constantly assisted. Instead of giving me complacency, my knowledge that I was never completely alone gave me both comfort and the confidence I needed to take matters into my own hands.

I began to inspect, what I expect.

It saddens me that people feel guilty for expecting more. Why is this the case? Why do they feel uncomfortable if they *expect* more success? Why do they dial back on that verb and replace it with a less aggressive one like "hope?"

The meaning completely changes when you *hope* for more success, or *hope* for better health, or *hope* to improve your financial situation. You give up all involvement and responsibility. You just give up.

There are times when hope has a place in your life and your spiritual and mental process. One never wants to lose hope for your child's continued happiness in life or hope for world peace.

There is a place for hope.

When it comes to your success and things over which you can or could have input and control, you need to **expect**.

My expectations are the basis of my success. Despite the hardships in my life, I can honestly tell you with unwavering confidence I have *never* just been satisfied with what I have so far.

I wake up every day expecting success.

I wish this were an audio book so you could hear the passion in my voice in the words that you are reading right now: I have never entertained a lifestyle of decrease; I have never thought to myself, "this is it." You absolutely, without question deserve your achievements and there is nothing wrong with waking up every day expecting exactly that!

Sashin Governor is a prime example of someone who internalized the concept of expectation at a young age. He accompanied his father to my seminars before he was a teenager, and he was not a shy, self-conscious 12-year old. Sashin sat up front and gave me every ounce of his attention. He put my teachings to work as soon as he was able and hit his first million by the time he was 20. Now, at 23, he is a multimillionaire and speaks on stages around the world.

As he was getting started, he called me almost every day. He never had a little voice in the back of his head that told him that he was bothering me, that it was too many phone calls, that he needed to dial it back. I recognized his hunger and mindset and I gave him direct access whenever he wanted.

Sashin was very young when he heard the concept *expectation to increase*. He was not jaded or tired; he hadn't grown up with limitations on his future. He knew that if he focused on limitation, that's what he would get.

He works like he is broke, every day, and he never stops to count his successes or rest on his laurels. Because he internalizes his expectation to increase, he's growing exponentially, and he'll have his first million-dollar year within two years.

There is so much power in *expectation*. Getting you to the mindset of expecting results will catapult you into a life that most people only dream of having. I want you to get to the mindset and determination of success in the exact same way that when you take a breath you *expect* oxygen, the exact same way that you *expect* a chair to hold you up when you sit down, the exact same way you *expect* the electricity to work when you turn on the lights.

You need to have that exact same expectation for personal triumph. Every day of your life you should wake up with an expectation of success.

It can start for you now. Inspect what you expect! Everyday, *expect* increase and I promise you, *your personal Break Through is imminent!*

Biography

Johnny Wimbrey is a speaker, author, trainer, and motivator, working with sales teams, high-profile athletes, politicians, and personalities around the world.

He has launched three companies—Wimbrey Training Systems, Wimbrey Global, and Royal Success Club International—and heads a sales team of thousands in more than 50 countries, overseeing an active customer database of half a million families.

Johnny shares his powerful message through speaking engagements around the world. He also has a wide media following and has appeared as a guest expert and panelist on television shows including the *Steve Harvey Show, E! News,* and *The Today Show.*

Johnny's first book, *From the Hood to Doing Good,* has sold more than 200,000 copies in printed and digital editions.

Johnny has collaborated on several other books including *Conversations of Success* and *Multiple Streams of Determination;* combined, they have more than 500,000 copies in print.

Johnny regularly speaks for non-profit organizations and reunites children with their families from whom they've been separated for years due to government action. He and his wife, Crystal, are co-founders of Wimbrey WorldWide Ministries, a non-profit which has built six schools in Central America and helped fund water purification systems in Africa.

Contact Information:

Johnny D. Wimbrey
Master Motivation/Success Trainer

Most Requested Topics:
Motivation/Keynote
Overcoming Adversity
Youth Enrichment
Leadership/Sales

www.johnnywimbrey.com

 @Wimbrey

 @Wimbrey

 @Wimbrey

 Johnny Wimbrey

 @Wimbrey

 LinkedIn@Wimbrey

CHAPTER TWO

You've Been Picked, Not Picked On

Willie Myers

It didn't feel like I was dreaming. I wasn't awake though I could hear voices and what sounded like a faint beeping sound, but I couldn't wake up. I heard someone say, "He's moving." Why were people in my apartment?

As I began to open my eyes, it was so bright I felt a burning sensation so I squeezed them closed. A voice said, "Willie, just relax." I slowly tried to open them again.

This time I noticed I was in an all-white room; monitors were on the wall and a hissing sound came from a ventilator. As a paramedic, I recognized my surroundings, but they made no sense.

Wait! Then it hit me; I was in a hospital. But how and why was I here? The last thing I remembered was swimming in the Mediterranean just outside the U.S. Embassy in Tel Aviv, Israel.

As I continued to wake up, I became aware of excruciating pain in my neck and shoulder. I realized a breathing tube was coming out of my right nostril and a ventilator was controlling my breathing.

"Willie, you were in an accident."

"You were brought here by ambulance because you drowned. You were pulled from the water and they did CPR on you."

The back of my head was pounding; I knew I suffered some kind of closed-head injury. I tried to remember my kids' birthday's and names. Cool . . .my long-term memory was intact.

My nose was itching, so I tried to use my left hand to scratch my nose but my arm wouldn't move. I tried to move my right hand, but my right shoulder was killing me, so I looked back down at my left hand and tried to move it again. It wouldn't move. Maybe they had restrained me. Maybe I was combative; why else would I be restrained? And why was I wearing a cervical collar around my neck?

But my arms weren't moving. I looked down at my legs and tried to move them. They weren't moving either.

I realized I was a quadriplegic. *Oh, God,* I thought pleadingly, and I began to sob.

How was I injured? I couldn't remember anything. Wait! I remembered I was swimming but no details; my memory was fuzzy.

The doctor said I was pulled from the Mediterranean in cardiac arrest two days before; they performed CPR on the beach and all the way to the hospital; I was revived in the emergency room. They took me for an MRI, and discovered my neck was broken at the C-4 region and there was pressure on my spinal cord. I had emergency surgery to relieve the pressure and woke up two days later.

I'd been a paramedic in some aspect of public safety for twenty-one years before I was recruited to work overseas as a civilian contractor in 2005. I served as a member of the Department of State's Diplomatic Security Service, part of the U.S. Consulate's protection detail in Jerusalem. My job title was *Protective Security Specialist Paramedic.* I had arrived in Israel two months earlier from Afghanistan, where I worked in Kabul from 2008 to 2014 on the embassy's protection detail and personnel recovery and hostage rescue team. Prior to that, I worked for three years in Baghdad, Iraq, as a member of the Ambassador's protection detail. I'd helped protect Presidents George W. Bush and Barack Obama.

I've always had a Type-A personality, very direction-orientated, expecting things to be done exactly the way I wanted. Now the life that I had worked so hard for was gone.

I was a quadriplegic, and I still had no idea what had happened to me.

I learned the next week when the man responsible for saving my life visited me in my hospital room. He'd visited earlier but I had been unconscious.

My rescuer was at the beach with his family when he saw me, this big muscular guy who looked as though I was there on a purpose. As a former medic with the Israeli Defense Force, he assumed I worked for the U.S. Embassy right there on the edge of the beach.

He saw me swim out toward a rock face about 100 meters off the beach, and because I was swimming alone, he kept his eye on me. (My swim was part of my PT fitness readiness preparation; I swam 200 meters once a week, ran six miles once a week, and worked out in the gym twice a week. Yes, I was in shape!)

What he didn't know was that I had decided to cut my swim short because the current was so rough and choppy. On my way back, the current was so strong it pushed me against a buoy line. I figured no big deal, I would just hold onto the line and pull myself back to shore.

I'd made it almost back to the beach—only 30 feet out with my feet touching the ocean floor—and that was the last thing I remember. Four years after the accident, that's my only memory of September 26, 2014, the date that would change my life forever.

I was medically evacuated back to the States in two weeks, and many emotions were going through my head during the flight home. Would I ever walk again? What would my life be like?

The Shepherd Center in Atlanta, Georgia, one of the top spinal rehab facilities in the country, was my home for the next three months while I regained minimal movement to my arms and legs. I was released in late January 2015, and my outpatient physical therapy continued another seven months until the company I worked for stopped my insurance.

Yeah, they canceled my insurance because I wasn't working. In March 2016, Fox 5 News in Atlanta did an investigative report on my story. Thanks to their story, the Shadows Warriors Project reached out to me a month later and they made it possible for me to return to the Shepherd Center for my rehab.

Fox 5 Atlanta has the story on their website; they helped me more than they knew. Six months later, I won my Workers' Compensation case and things looked up even more.

But, as we know, when there are ups, there are downs. I was reminded of this a few months later when I came home after a trip.

I landed safely at the airport in Atlanta, retrieved my bags, and met my van driver, who helped secure my wheelchair. I remember leaving the airport, and that was it. For a second time, I lost two days from my life.

The van driver had become concerned when I stopped talking with him. I didn't respond when he tried to wake me, so he called 9-1-1. Paramedics arrived and checked my blood sugar, and it was over 600.

I woke up two days later. My mouth was so dry, my body was weak. What was going on? The doctor came in and told me that I had been in a diabetic coma. How was that possible? I was always healthy and suddenly I'm a Type II diabetic?

There's a saying that events happen in threes, and I was not disappointed. A couple weeks later, my wife unlocked the door for my caregiver, who was scheduled to arrive at seven a.m. Instead of leaving as she usually did, my wife sat down next to my bed and looked at me.

"I didn't sign up for this. I filed for divorce," she told me.

"Okay, thanks," I said quietly while looking at her.

What else was there to say? She'd filed for divorce. A week later, a sheriff's deputy served me with divorce papers in our living room. That was event number three. I sat in my wheelchair and I cried.

That night while I was lying in bed, a feeling of deep calm came over me. I wasn't worried, I wasn't distraught, I was in a peaceful state. I had a discussion with God and said, "Whatever this is, whatever your will is for me, I submit to you. I submit to your will. And whatever this is, let's get it done."

By this time, I'd been back in rehab at the Shepherd Center just less than a year, and I had taken some assisted steps, nothing independent at this point. Now I asked my physical therapist to help me climb three steps. And he did. But we didn't just climb three steps, we climbed an entire flight of stairs.

I used my divorce as motivation to *not* stay where my ex-wife-to-be expected me to stay. A couple of months later, I rented a two-story house for the sole purpose of climbing upstairs and conditioning myself. I had limitations, for sure, but I accepted my challenges and took them on. I was focused and determined to walk again. There were many who watched my journey and supported me, including my children, who never gave up on me.

One person to whom I give particular thanks is my friend Patricia; she's been instrumental to my recovery, and I believe she came into my life for that reason.

I made a point of surrounding myself with positive people, positive thinking, and positive expectations. Up to that point in my life, I hadn't questioned or even thought much about my mindset. I was aware I was stubborn and determined, and I'd always used that to my benefit when I could, but it took the accident and what would follow before I realized the effect my journey would have on other people.

Mindset is defined as "the established set of attitudes held by someone." And that is exactly what I had to have—a focused attitude. The breakthrough to finding your mindset comes from accepting your challenges and allowing those challenges to help mold you. You must be willing to accept it and not find excuses or blame others for not meeting your challenge head on.

Don't get me wrong—your challenge is going to suck, and it's going to be whatever puts you on your knees. Rebuilding yourself first begins when *you* decide *to win.*

Let's review my situation. I was told I would never walk

again; my body was as good as it was going to get. I have a letter from my doctor that declared I was at maximum recovery. At that moment, I began to change my mindset. I used the doctor's letter as the foundation of my change like someone would use newspaper to line the bottom of a bird cage, if you catch my analogy.

I sustained a C-4 central spinal cord contusion, not a severed spinal cord, which would have been much worse. Knowing my recovery began with physical therapy, I simply looked at my options. I could push myself beyond what my physical therapist would do or I could simply quit. Though quitting is easy, it was never really an option.

I deleted any aspect of failure from my options, just wiped it out of my mind. I wouldn't allow failure to live there.

Next, I separated myself from negative people, even those I loved. My drive, what I wanted, and where my vision was directed were different than their goals and visions. You can't have negativity affecting your growth or success. When those close to you try to hold you back, it's not healthy to you or your future.

If you complain a lot, if you take no responsibility for your actions, if you quit something because it gets hard? Then I can't give you my attention.

That's what you must do. First, strengthen your own foundation before you can help someone else. If they're not even willing to try, then you're already behind the curve.

I knew I couldn't quit. I understood where I was physically and mentally. I pushed myself to work harder, so much so, that even my kids could see what was happening. It became clear to them that no matter what their circumstances, they too could use their situation as a vessel to improve who they were and ideally use it to help someone else, too.

Personal development was a new animal to me. Though I'd heard of Les Brown and Tony Robbins, of course, until then I didn't think I needed their help in *my* life. All facets of my life had been going well—my career, my health, and my family, or so I thought. There was a *lot* I had to learn after I was injured and all three facets of that "perfect" life were irrevocably changed. I accepted my life had to change so I could help others.

And I'm OK with that. If this is how God wants to use me, then let's do this.

Whatever *your* challenge is on your journey, it's there to help you grow. A sudden job loss, relationship loss, a major health scare or loss. In my case, I got all three challenges.

So how do you adapt your mindset to recover from strike one, or two, or three?

It's simple: *Own it.* First see where you want to go before you take your first step to recover from where you are. Realize it's not going to happen overnight; that's the hardest part of the journey.

We have a path in life, a direction of travel, if you will. That path is filled with some obstacles, even some roadblocks, and your path will change direction. Sometimes it goes backward and you may have to start over, and that's okay, too.

The most important thing is to *never stop.* It's easy to become discouraged; it's even easier to quit—though you'll regret that forever. To keep going, you must have a focus, something you can really see—your **WHY** (What-Hurts-You).

My **WHY** is my kids. I'm doing everything that I can do to become a better version of the person I used to be. Anything that I do from here on out creates a legacy for them.

Here's my approach:

I'm not afraid of failing, I've got nothing to lose. In my mindset, there's no such thing as failure. Failure is just a task that hasn't been accomplished yet. It's up to you to find out how to accomplish your task, not to give up because it's hard or because someone said you'd fail. You have a problem the moment that you allow somebody else's opinion of you to dictate your future. That's when you've lost.

The good thing is that somebody's opinion of you doesn't define where you are going. You can always change. Change isn't so much reinventing yourself as it is discovering who you really are and strengthening yourself from the inside—and that comes from personal development. So, don't be so close-minded because it will keep you from growing and you'll fall behind.

Realize this: *You are worth it.* This is the single most important concept you must understand; you must know deep down in your heart that you are worth the effort involved, you are worth the pain it will take to get to where you want to be in life.

Accept every challenge that comes to you. Don't be **POOR** (Passing Over Opportunities Repeatedly) minded; only *you* know where you are in life. If what you're doing isn't working and the people with whom you surround yourself don't support you, what then? Then realize you might be doing it wrong.

One of my mentors said something that really resonated with me: "**Surround yourself around the thinking that outthinks you.**" I wish I had been taught this in school; it would have been more helpful than studying the War of 1812. I know it doesn't make much sense when you first see it—it looks like a misquote—but accept it and it'll help sustain you.

Your hopes, your dreams, your aspirations are all yours and you only get one shot at this thing called life. Just because an obstacle or a challenge presents itself, it doesn't mean you've lost any opportunity to be where you envisioned yourself.

Perseverance is an investment of will and determination. Remember, success is earned, not given. Too many feel they are entitled and want others to invest in that entitlement behavior and then get upset when they are denied.

Understand that when you're accomplishing your goals, they're not going to come easy. There will be failure, but failure is just a task that hasn't yet been accomplished.

Personal development is the key to your interior and exterior growth. Once you decide you can create and be the owner of your own life, then your growth will begin. Don't focus on the "right here, right now" . . . first make the decision that you will meet your roadblocks head on, one by one.

I recommend two books to help you on your journey: *From the Hood to Doing Good*, by Johnny Wimbrey, and *Awaken the Giant Within*, by Anthony Robbins

I can't tell you how long your journey will take. I don't know your beliefs or if you read the Bible, but Galatians 6:9 can be helpful to us all: *And let us not grow weary of doing good, for in due season we will reap,* **if we do not give up.**

You have a choice to make; it's your decision and your journey. Only you know if your dreams and goals are worth it. But if you allow *FEAR* (which is nothing but False Evidence Appearing Real) to stop you from having the life you're meant to have, you'll live in regret.

Let's make your life count.

Biography

Willie Myers was born in Philadelphia, Pennsylvania, and feels privileged to have been reared and loved, along with his three brothers and one stepsister, by two amazing parents, Willie J. Myers, Sr., and Emma L. Myers. He lost his mother to a drunken driver when he was only seven and was raised in Texas after her death. His father died when he was nineteen.

When he graduated from high school in 1984, Willie became an EMT-Paramedic at Texas College of Osteopathic Medicine in Ft. Worth, Texas.

He lives in Atlanta, a divorced father of six wonderful children: four daughters, Emily, Kandis, Monica, and Sydni, and two sons, Alexander and Logan.

Contact Information:

Facebook Page: Willie Myers
Instagram: Williejmyers
Twitter: @williejmyers

CHAPTER THREE

Don't Waste Your Life

Teresa Thomas

This is for all of the teenage girls who would never reach out to a shelter for battered women, to a friend, to her parents, to a school counselor, or to anyone for that matter. This is for that isolated girl in an apartment waiting for God to show up and rescue her.

Sometimes, when I begin to think about what I went through, tears start flowing down my cheeks—the type of tears you just cannot stop. When a co-worker asks if anything is wrong, I simply lie, "I read a really bad case."

From the outside looking in, my life seems great now. I have a Bachelor's in Human Development, a Master's in Social Work, and a Certificate in Criminal Justice. I review child abuse and neglect cases. I also teach at a local top-ten university. I am happily married with two adorable girls. What you don't see on the inside is someone who went through hell and came out *alive*.

Where do I begin? *Should* I tell my story to help other women?

Teenage Love

I was a typical teenage girl who loved boys and New Kids on the Block. I wasn't from a broken home. I lived in a middle-class family with three siblings and two married and sometimes happy parents.

You see, it really doesn't matter what type of family you come from. Anyone can become a victim of these two textbook words I didn't know existed even when I was in the middle of it—*domestic violence.* Who came up with these two words in the first place? Just call it what it is, for God's sake. He beat the shit out of you, right?

My self-esteem slowly dropped inch by inch throughout my childhood years and then into adulthood. It started in fifth grade, when I was bullied into joining the mean girls, and in turn I was embarrassed for not standing up for my friends.

Fast forward to when I fell hard for Chase in eighth grade. He was a popular boy with a perfect sense of humor and a big flirt, and he knew exactly what to say to me. He could also be the biggest a-hole on planet Earth.

As I think back now, I question almost all the decisions I made about boys when I was a teenager. I get the whole "father/daughter" complex, but I was close with my dad. He was always there for me.

I am not sure I really ever had a "great" relationship with my mom. I was the bull-headed, middle child who always gave her a hard time. I am sure my mom did not enjoy our constant battles; maybe that is why I slowly detached myself from her emotionally and physically.

The Beginning of Real-life HELL

My knight in shining armor arrived when I was 16 and he was 19 years old. I met Reggie through friends. Reggie was so charismatic, the life of the party; everyone either looked up to him or they were deathly afraid of him. He took control of the room with his sense of humor, his laugh, and his wit. I was instantly hooked.

The night I met Reggie, I was at a house party in Madison. I had just left another party where my ex-boyfriend, Chase, and I had been arguing until he hit me in my eye with the blunt side of a meat cleaver.

One of my girlfriends hid Chase in the backseat of her car as we drove to the next party. After we arrived, when I told my new crush Reggie about the stowaway, he forced him to leave. I felt safe and fell completely in love, head over heels fast. Little did I know that he would try to kill me several times over.

The Dismissal of Abuse

"Teri, guess who *I'm* with?" Jessica said, so flippantly I knew something was going on.

"Who?"

"Reggie and Zadie."

Was she toying with me? I became furious and hopped into the car my dad gave me on my 16th birthday, just a few months before.

When I saw Jessica's car, she sped up. Mind you, this was my friend. Why was she making me chase her? We were both weaving in and out of traffic until she finally stopped and Reggie got out of the car, yelling until he got close enough to slap me. I crashed into Zadie's mouth, gashing my forehead.

Jessica left with Reggie, and all I could feel was utter shock. I was crying hysterically, confused and hurt.

"He's never hit me before. Where do you guys want to be dropped off? I'm going to go see him." . . . and that was the beginning.

"I knew you'd come back," he said when I pulled up.

"After what you just did, why would you think I'd come back?"

He smiled.

"I don't know why you were acting that way. I wasn't cheating on you. I love you Teri," he said.

Reggie wrapped his muscular arms around me and that's all I needed to hear: "I love you."

They say the brain changes when you suffer trauma. Humans hit with trauma are transformed into Play-Doh—they are reshaped and their thought patterns change.

The next two years were constant trauma. Sometimes I'd count the days in between getting hit in the face or locked in a closet or suffocated with a pillow. I thought what I suffered was not abuse because he never used a closed fist. The rest of the time he was still my knight in shining armor. He'd take care of me when I was sick. He'd make sure I got to work on time and would be waiting for me when I got off.

The next time Reggie hit me in front of people, we were all in his back bedroom smoking weed. And then smack, smack, hit, smack again. His friends were all laughing at me.

This is when I started to feel real shame, yet I did nothing to stop it. I wasn't tied down physically to him, I didn't live with him, but he had me mentally fixated.

The violence escalated, as it always does. Reggie hit me so

violently that broken blood vessels would appear all over my face. He'd grab me so hard and force my face into a pillow until I couldn't breathe. He'd push me into the closet and kick and hit me until he had enough.

If I took showers by myself, I'd get beaten. If I asked him a question he didn't like, I'd get hit. If I looked a certain way at him, I'd get slapped. He'd force me to only look at the ground when we were out at bars. One time, I was beaten badly because a guy remembered me from where I worked.

Another time, Reggie dragged me across the floor by my hair after he'd beaten me at his friend's home because he thought I had flirted with his friend. The police were called and pictures were taken. The local domestic violence shelter told me they had no beds available and I ended up sleeping in my car because I was too afraid to go home.

My body and mind were always on high alert. It's all I thought about. I was completely and utterly consumed by what would happen next. Sometimes, I wondered where all of his rage came from. The only thing that ever made him stop was my saying, "I love you. I'll never leave you."

I was barely 17, and the day I graduated from high school, I moved out of my parent's house and rented a room from a good friend. Reggie moved in, too. As I look back, there were good days. Reggie was charismatic, funny, strong, and sensitive—all of the qualities I fell madly in love with. He told me every day how much he loved me.

I found out Reggie fathered a baby right out of school; he met me when he was finishing up a year of probation for abusing the mother of his child.

I tried to leave Reggie a few times. On one particular night, I told him over the phone we were done, and then I headed home with my friend Jessica, who'd moved into the basement of the house where I was living along with her boyfriend, Anthony.

"OMG!" We saw headlights flick on in the driveway at our house. Anthony had parked facing out so that he could easily pull out and maneuver. When we didn't turn in, Anthony and Reggie began chasing us. I was deathly afraid as I wove in and out of traffic, knowing that if I stopped I would be beaten until I hyperventilated.

I eventually saw a police car, pulled over and told the police officer what was going on. Reggie saw me talking to the police as they drove past. I knew I was in trouble.

When Jessica and I pulled up to the house, Anthony's car wasn't in sight. I walked into the house and there was Reggie. He grabbed my hair, slapped my face, and bashed me into the window. I felt like a rag doll, getting hit so many times I could no longer count, crying hysterically, pleading with him to stop. And here was the magic phrase again—"I love you. Please. I'll never leave you, Reggie."

He stopped. "Now go take a bath and clean up." And that was it. I survived, but my emotional capacity to feel anything was dying.

Of course, that wasn't the last time. He soon broke my nose and sprained my arm. I went back to him with my arm in a sling. I felt trapped. I believed that if I left, he would kill me.

"I'm going to go away for a long time if you don't go to my probation agents and tell them you lied," he told me. That was his crazy way of dealing with my broken nose and sprained arm.

At that time (and for years to come), I was too ashamed to tell my story. I felt people would judge me, and I was paralyzed by fear. If you could imagine yourself as a character in the scariest movie you've ever seen that seemed to last forever—that's what I was feeling.

"Ok, I'll do it," I told him. "I'll tell them that I was jealous and I made the whole story up. I'll tell them I got hurt in a car accident."

As I was telling my made-up story to the probation agents, I knew they knew I was lying. They knew I was covering up for Reggie but couldn't prove it. I was the victim and recanted it all.

No More Abuse

Late one cold night I was irritated because Reggie told me to come get him at a friend's, and I was waiting and waiting. I went into his friend's house to ask, "Are you ready to go?"

Reggie gave me the look of death. Another friend, Cliff, asked us for a ride home. As soon as Reggie sat in the passenger seat, he started hitting me, and my head banged the driver's side window with every blow.

Finally, Cliff interjected, "Reggie, stop hitting her. She's driving. You don't want us to get into an accident!"

Reggie told me to drive to our apartment, and he took my car to drive Cliff home. I knew when he came back I'd be beaten and suffocated in the closet.

It was too much to bear. I had been beaten all the way home. I was bleeding. I was done. Something switched in my brain.

Have you ever just made a split second decision that completely changed your life? You can. I did. I knew my body couldn't take another beating. My brain was damaged, I was terrified, but I had the courage to call my parents.

It was past midnight, but my mom answered. Thank God. I

told her where to pick me up; I'd be hiding in the bushes until I saw her car. I gathered a few things and ran. My heart was pumping so fast, it almost jumped out of my chest.

My mom rescued me.

Starting Over, but Not Really

I testified against Reggie. I was all alone. He winked at me while I was on the stand. It felt as if he and I were the only ones in the courtroom that day. He knew what he'd done to me. I no longer had physical bruises, but the emotional scars cut extremely deep. Reggie ended up receiving a five-year sentence for several batteries, false imprisonment, intimidating a victim, and operating my vehicle without my consent. A part of me felt very guilty for sending him to prison. Another part of me felt safe. I could breathe again. The monster was behind bars.

After the trial, I was evicted from my apartment, and ended up sleeping in my car and crashing on many couches.

It took me awhile to get straightened up. When my friends said, "Teri, let's go out," my answer was "yes" every single time. When I couldn't financially keep up with my partying lifestyle, I started to steal. I used drugs and I started drinking very heavily. Professionals would say I was "self-medicating" to mask the pain in my heart.

Moving Forward

I met Isaiah once Reggie was in jail. He had been in and out of prison, but the moment I met him we connected. He became my best friend with no benefits, and I instantly felt safe around this felon. As I look back now, I don't know if I would have remained strong if Isaiah hadn't come into my life. It's as if God ordered that to happen. Isaiah ended up going back to prison and our relationship eventually faded.

Then I moved from one brief relationship to the next, and one actually almost landed *me* in prison. I was smuggling marijuana in balloon bags into the prison system while visiting another felon for whom I'd fallen in love. I was also stealing and ended up in jail. I took the First Offenders Program and volunteered at a parenting class for low-income mothers and their children. I had to write several papers on stealing and the repercussions to society.

I was not only embarrassed by what I had done, but I also understood the impact it had on others. I vowed to do better with my life. I started to feel the power of karma. What you put into this world, you get back tenfold.

When I turned 21 and pregnant with my first child, Jada, I started to truly think about my life. Jada changed the direction of it. Something clicked in my head as it did the cold winter night two years before when I left Reggie. I looked around at work and thought, "I don't want to be one of these women in their 60s making minimum wage."

I applied to a local college, took two classes at night and fell in love with learning. When I transferred to the top-ten university where I now work, I felt out of place, but at the same time, I knew I was in my element. My fellow classmates went to their dorms and I went home to my Section 8 apartment filled with rats and roaches to take care of my one-year old daughter while I finished papers and tried to study.

When my relationship with Jada's father dissolved, I moved forward with my life. I pursued social work because I enjoyed the class material more than other courses I had taken. As I learned about child abuse, neglect, domestic violence, and human growth and behavior, I think my path was already dictated by God. I just had to connect the dots.

For the next several years my focus was Jada and college, and I was hypervigilant on what I wanted in a relationship. Then and now, I talk to Jada about not losing herself in a relationship, and to enter and stay in it for the right reasons. I practiced what I preached. I increased my self-worth through exercising, practicing forgiveness, and helping others realize their potentials.

Eventually, a close friend played matchmaker. I checked the guy out to make sure he had no convictions for batteries against women. I was no longer willing to accept anything less than a great man with good, sound morals.

My husband is a tall, handsome man who has a faith-based background and took on Jada as his own. Over the last several years, we have been on a quest for personal growth, which helped me overcome and heal from my past trauma and abandonment. I used to think personal development was "drinking the Kool-Aid." Now, it is a part of my daily life.

For 25 years, I have lived my life as a survivor and I am still growing. If we aren't changing in our lives emotionally, physically, or professionally, we are simply dying a slow death.

I teach my students that we can change the direction of our lives. I teach my colleagues that every day is a new day to put positive energy into the world. If I can go through hell and live to tell my story to allow others to feel empowered to share their stories, why can't you, too? We all have the ability within us to create a ripple effect.

I would be disrespecting God if I didn't share my mess to give you this message. It wouldn't be fair to all of the women—both current victims and future survivors. #messtomessage

Biography

Teresa was born and raised in the Midwest in the small town of Oregon, Wisconsin. A survivor of domestic violence as a teenager, she is a strong believer that there is no testimony without a TEST.

For most of her adult life, Teresa has worked in the field of social work. She is an instructor at the University of Wisconsin-Madison, and she reviews child abuse and neglect cases for the state of Wisconsin.

Teresa is happily married with two beautiful daughters.

Contact Information:

Email: tjclarkthomas@me.com

Facebook:@iamterithomas

Instagram:@teresa.j.thomas

CHAPTER FOUR

Respect Yourself

Eric Luther Ingram

It was early evening on Saturday, September 15, 2018, and I was heading home after spending a great afternoon watching my oldest nephew, Kenny Knight, Jr., play college football against the Indiana Hoosiers.

Kenny Jr. is a senior at Ball State University in Muncie, Indiana. Ken's brother, James "Jimmy Jam" Knight, is a sophomore playing for the Fighting Illini at the University of Illinois and is doing very well for himself as well. Their respective teams, the Cardinals and Illini, both played that day. Some of the family went to Soldier Field in Chicago to see Jimmy Jam, while the others, including me, traveled to Muncie to see Kenny Jr. We were all on our cell phones throughout the day trying to find out who was where, what was going on, and who scored.

It was not just another day for the family; it was game day!

I had dropped my cousin, Marc, and his wife, Michelle, off at their house and was heading home to grab my bag before I caught a flight to Las Vegas to see a middleweight fight. Before I got home, I was waved through a sobriety checkpoint, as were a few vehicles in line behind me. I was stopped about a quarter-mile down the road at a stoplight when my cousin called me to say he'd left his medication in my vehicle. The light was still red and I was on the car's hands-free Bluetooth with him, so I reached down onto the passenger side of the floor to pick up his medication.

As I was reaching down, a Dodge Ram pickup truck driven by a drunk driver came out of nowhere and slammed into the back of my Cadillac sedan. Because of the way I was hit, I was trapped in the car and the only thing that saved me from truly serious injury and possible death was the fact that I had reached down to pick up my cousin's medication. The doctor said that if I still had been sitting up, my neck probably would have been broken in the crash.

After the truck struck my vehicle, I could hear my cousin yelling and screaming into his phone trying to figure out what was going on. At the same time, my OnStar communication system turned on and the operator was also calling my name repeatedly. My cousin says that I kept saying, "I'm dying, I'm dying," but I can't remember that. I was going in and out of consciousness. What I do recall is a vivid flashback to forty years ago.

I was in sixth grade and playing soccer in the Catholic Youth Organization League back in Cahokia, Illinois. I saw myself running up and down the soccer field with my teammates. My parents, other parents, and the rest of the crowd cheered us on. Their faces were so clear in the flashback that it seemed as though I could reach out and touch them. I even watched as I drank water during a timeout and stood on the sidelines discussing a play with my coach.

Thinking about it afterward, the crash was scary and troubling. Recognizing that you nearly died is humbling and unsettling. I spent one day in the hospital and was told to stay home and rest for a couple of days until the test results came back. When the results came back negative, I was told I could go back to work, but light duty only. My insurance company gave me a rental car and all was well, so I thought.

On the day I went back to work, I was hit from behind while

crossing the Mississippi River. Being hit twice in such a short period was mind-blowing to me. When I was hit the second time, I kept saying to myself that my parents left me here to finish what they had started, and I could not die before it gets done. Four months later, I am still under a doctor's care. There are attorneys involved and the other driver in the first crash is facing criminal charges.

I do not believe it is possible to go through two major car accidents in such a short period of time and not do some self-reflecting. Am I where I should be? Am I doing all the things I need and want to do? Am I showing myself respect and representing my family in the best way possible? Am I making my way or simply marking time?

My father was a major rhythm and blues (soul) singer in the late 1960s and 1970s. Between 1969 and 1987, nineteen of his songs were on the Billboard Rhythm and Blues (R&B) and Pop Music charts. His signature song, *If Loving You Is Wrong, I Don't Want to be Right*, made it to #1 on the R&B and #3 on the Pop charts in 1972. The song remained there for 18 weeks and sold four million copies. He would go on to become an important artist and musical sensation.

My father was also a significant songwriter. He wrote classics such as *Missing You, Help Me Love*, and the crowd favorite, *Ain't That Loving You, For More Reasons Than One*. Then in 1971, my dad co-wrote *Respect Yourself*, the largest selling single in the history of Stax Records. My dad wrote the song to express his discontent with society at the time. In 2002, the song was inducted into the Grammy Hall of Fame, and in 2010, it was ranked on the *Rolling Stone* magazine list of the *500 Greatest Songs of All Time*.

My dad preached respecting yourself almost daily. He would say, "Respect yourself and represent the family in the utmost fashion." He believed it and he lived it. After two major car crashes, I found myself wondering if I was doing all that I could to follow my father's wishes.

A family member once told me that when a parent dies too soon, the child spends the rest of their life trying to make them proud. Well, it has been double duty for me because I lost both parents within a 17-month period. My father passed in March 2007 and my mother followed in August 2008. My father had been ill with diabetes, kidney failure, and partial blindness, and my mother had spent her final years caring for him prior to his death. That much loss in a short period can be overwhelming, but I had to gather myself and my thoughts.

To some, my childhood and adolescence might have seemed a bit "bourgeois" or "privileged." Not everyone had a father who would pick his son and his friends up in a limousine and drive them to school on the day after a concert in our city. But my parents were regular people. My mother was a government worker who helped people wrongfully discharged from employment. She taught me about negotiating and dealing with people. To most of the world, my dad was a star, but to our family he was just "Dee" or "Lu T" (short for Luther Thomas). He taught me many things, including how to speak in front of large groups of people confidently.

Growing up in my East St. Louis neighborhood was a wonderful and safe experience. Everyone treated each other like family. When my friends and I went outside to play, we got dirty, playing games or racing each other in the street. If someone had a fight, then that's what it was, a fist fight. Kids did not have guns back then. When the street lights came on, it was my reminder to be in the front yard by curfew. School was mandatory and we were careful with our language, not only around our elders, but our teachers as well. Talking back was out of the question. There were rules and breaking them meant big trouble.

I went to a Catholic school and was involved in all sports, but soccer was the sport in which I excelled. My soccer skills earned me a ton of awards and carried over into high school where I was deemed one of the best players in the area.

Learning how to kick a soccer ball eventually lead to my ability to kick a football. I entered the National Football League (NFL) Punt, Pass, and Kick Contest and won. I was sponsored by one of the local car dealerships in town. The president of the dealership accompanied me and my parents on the plane to Pontiac, Michigan, where I was to perform in front of more than 50,000 people at the Pontiac Silverdome while representing my city's NFL team, the St. Louis Cardinals.

For years, I had watched my father perform in front of thousands of people, and now at age 13, I was about to do the same. I can still, until this day remember him coaching me and getting me ready to compete at halftime of the Lions/49ers game. It was also the moment when I got a taste of what he went through constantly. My attitude changed after that. From then on, I knew things would be expected of me and I would have to rise to the occasion.

My college years were also some of the best years of my life. It was the first time I had new friends and met people from across the United States and around the globe. Thanks to those friends, I was introduced to new foods, new cultures, and new ideas. I began to make my own way and figure out who I was and what I wanted to do, as we all need to do at that age.

People knew me because of my father, and that got my friends and me into concerts for free. I can remember going to see rap, rock, and reggae shows all in the same week. I was getting into pre-show sound checks, and post-show backstage access became a regular thing. It was all new and exciting to me.

In the early '90s, I started managing my first rock group. In 1995, I helped manage a promising local rap group, which at the time looked like it was going to be the next big thing in music. I met a lot of major players in the music industry, like Sean "Puffy" Combs, Russell Simmons, and Michael "Blue" Williams. Williams would go on to manage Outkast, which would eventually become the biggest rap group in the world.

I met entertainers like comedian/host Steve Harvey and movie director/producer John Singleton, who used my father's music in his 2005 film, *Hustle and Flow*. A pivotal moment in my life came when one of my mentors, the late Afeni Shakur, sat on her back porch and shared some advice with me, the same advice that she gave her son, the legendary Tupac Shakur. Her advice helped me grow in the business as well as in life.

But for all the famous people and connections, striking out on your own to make an impact on the world is what truly matters. After feeling my own mortality thanks to those two car crashes and ruminating over my life, I decided to speed up my work on various projects and asked God for his help and guidance as I proceed.

My goal is to start and operate my own film and music production company. Money is a vital part of such an effort, but timing and relationships are just as important. It is the relationships that you build along the way that will eventually create the timing needed to bring the money.

One of the most important relationships I've developed is with Ms. Thany Por and her family. A former Cambodian refugee, Thany contacted me after reading a short story I had written about my dad and his career. Thany hoped to do the same thing for her family and contacted me for guidance. After hearing and learning about her family and the Khmer Rouge, I flew to Boston to meet her and her family.

As I sat outside in their backyard at one of many summer cookouts, I was amazed at the joy and happiness they shared despite their horrific struggle for survival during Cambodia's genocide. The stories they told were unimaginable and humbled me. For the last two years, I have pledged my time and vision to Thany and her family in order to bring their story to the masses. Thany and I have co-written and published a nonfiction work titled *The Unwatered Rose (A Khmer Woman's Journey to Freedom)* that details their struggles to survive in Cambodia and their escape. There are a lot of important stories out there featuring people who have so much to offer the rest of us and I want to help make that happen.

I am also working on a second project, *If Loving You Is Wrong, I Don't Want To Be Right (The Movie)*, a biopic film based on my father's life and career. It digs into his personal and professional relationships with Jimi Hendrix, Ike Turner, James Brown, and Muhammad Ali. It also highlights my father's time at Stax Records in Memphis, Tennessee, set against the tumultuous Civil Rights movement that took place at the same time the label was becoming a major force in music.

There is so much I want to do. And now that I have asked for God's help, I believe it will all happen. Everyone needs to have a dream. And as mine develops into reality, I plan to continue to pay attention, stay excited, and never quit.

Most of all, I want to follow my father's wishes and respect myself and all of the people who helped me to become who I am. That is what my father would have wanted for me and what I want for myself.

Biography

As the son of rhythm and blues (soul) singer/songwriter and Stax Records legend, Luther Ingram, Eric Luther Ingram (Eli) had a remarkable upbringing. He is presently developing a production company that will develop and produce books and movies.

His current projects include his book *The Unwatered Rose (A Khmer Women's Journey To Freedom)*, with a film to follow, and writing/producing *If Loving You Is Wrong, I Don't Want To Be Right (The Movie)*. Eric also manages his father's music catalog and is developing new arrangements of those songs.

Eric resides in O'Fallon, Illinois.

Contact Information:

Email: Luthermovie@gmail.com
Facebook: Eli Eric Luther
Instagram: eli_eric_luther
Twitter: Eli Luther Ingram
LinkedIn: Eli Eric Luther Ingram

CHAPTER FIVE

The Value of Mentors

Billy Womack

When I look back at every success that I have ever had in life, whether it is athletics, my military career, or later life, I realize I had a great coach. My first coach was my amazing father and I had others after him.

Early on, I did not realize coaches were mentors—I only looked at the sports aspect. But in any sport or any occupation, I believe you need a mentor and to surround yourself with people who are pushing you to that next level. For everything at which I have been successful, I have had a mentor or a coach who helped me maximize my talents.

When I was in high school, I was privileged to have two of the best basketball coaches possible—Donnie Branham and Jimmy Phelps. These guys mentored me into becoming Arkansas Player of the Year and being offered over 20 college athletic scholarships. My summer league coach, Coach Ripley, also coached Derek Fisher and Corliss Williamson, my teammates, who later won NBA championships.

Keith Wilsey, who coached me to state championships in both track and cross country and eventually to tryouts for the Olympics, pushed me on and off the track, not only to be a better athlete but a better person. He taught me humility and sportsmanship.

Coaches help push you, but competition drives you.

Michael Jordan is probably the greatest basketball player in the history of the NBA. Michael Jordan had a basketball coach, and he had a mentor. He always had people working with him, helping him improve. Jordan won six NBA championships and five Most Valuable Player awards, the most ever. He remains the only sports figure to ever hit $1 billion in earnings in the NBA or any other professional sport.

Jordan could not have done that alone.

Greatness comes with mentorship and coaching. No one, regardless of their field, can go out and perform at full capacity every single day without having someone to push them.

I was fortunate to have some good mentors early in my life and be able to recognize their value. After high school, I joined the U.S. Air Force, and while I was serving, I met some phenomenal individuals.

Rob Childers was one of my sergeants. He believed in me and mentored me through part of my military career. Childers was a big part of my success in the military.

Once I got out of the military, my first job was in telecommunications in Florida. During my job interview, my future boss, Teresa, told me the company would make it possible for me to be successful.

"Where do you see yourself in five years?" Teresa asked during my interview.

"I see myself sitting where you're sitting, advising other people to help them fulfill their dreams."

"Wow. That's pretty bold," Teresa said. "I don't really hear that too often."

"I am the hardest worker you will ever find. If you tell me how to get there, I will."

"If you really want to succeed, here's what you're going to have to do," she advised.

To me, that is mentorship in the nutshell.

Teresa outlined the extra steps I needed to master so I could excel within the company, and she explained I should put in extra hours above and beyond everyone else.

When I started the job, I had never worked in sales before. My mentors told me sales was not about going out and "selling somebody."

"Sales is about listening to what the customer needs and fulfilling those needs. That is how you will succeed at this," they told me.

I went home after work and studied until 10 or 11 p.m. every night. By the end of my first 90 days, I was among the top five sales reps in that region and in the top ten in the entire company, worldwide.

By the end of my first year in corporate America, I was named *Forbes 500 Rookie of the Year* for a multi-billion-dollar company and the number two salesman in the world. I never reached number one—but I reached number two.

Three months before the end of that first year, I reached out to the number one salesman to learn from him.

"What is it you are doing that nobody else is doing?" I asked. "I want to watch you, study you, and mimic you."

That is the secret—find that person who is successful and duplicate what they are doing.

So many people want to go out and recreate the wheel. If it's not working for everybody else, I'm not saying it won't work for you. I'm just saying there's an easier path and that path will lead you there a lot quicker.

After my first year with the telecommunications company,

one of my customers met with me and made a proposal.

"We've heard that you excelled in athletics," the customer told me. "We've heard you're phenomenal at selling. We'd like to bring you in to be a partner in an online sports marketing agency that we're building."

National Football League Hall of Famer Warren Sapp was going to be our first client.

The customer was two years older than me and driving a car that cost in the six-figure range.

I believe if you surround yourself with people who are at the level to which you aspire, they raise the bar for you and help you achieve that level of success.

Reading the book *Think and Grow Rich* by Napoleon Hill changed my life. It helped me make the decision to leave the secure six-figure income I'd built up as a 24-year-old to become an entrepreneur, because it opened my eyes as to what possibilities existed. So I left telecommunications and became a partner in my customer's new business.

Within two years, we had the number one online sports marketing agency in the world, with more than 45 professional athletes as clients.

All of this took me into a lifestyle I had never imagined. I started seeing a different side of the entertainment—the sports, the glimmer, and the glam. I took my eye off what was important and became involved with people who had lifestyles and values different from my own.

I was young, money was pouring in, and I decided to buy a nightclub in Tampa. That's where my downfall began. I made the mistake of venturing out into new waters without having a successful mentor.

Without that key person and focus in my life, I started

doing drugs, staying out partying, and traveling all over the place. I got into trouble for drugs about a year later and did some jail time, something of which I am not very proud, but it's an example from which everybody else should learn.

When the police put handcuffs on me and sat me in a cruiser, it was time for an epiphany. The reality was I was tired of living that lifestyle, so I was glad to see it come to an end, but I was mortified; I knew how it would affect my reputation. I had let people down. I had lied to my family and I was in a very dark place in my life.

Thankfully, I had my mother and God to talk to.

I did not know what my next steps would be. I just promised God if He gave me a second opportunity, I would find a way to help others going through the same experiences.

I read a lot of books while I was in jail and it helped me keep my focus. Everything I read told me that recovering would take perseverance and dedication. I knew I needed to nourish my mind and body to get out of the hole I was in.

More than 70% of people who go to jail stay in jail and I did not want to fall into that category.

When I got out, I applied for more than one hundred jobs. I had a great résumé with successful military service and corporate sales career. But none of that mattered. No one would hire me because of my criminal record.

It was very, very draining. My brother actually moved to Florida and helped me get a place to live. I could not even get an apartment because of my criminal background.

My other brother flew into town and started a business, and I went to work for him doing automotive paint chip repair. My first paycheck was for $76. It was very humbling and I could not afford to shop anywhere more expensive than the Dollar

Store. But I swore that no matter what it was going to take, I was going to get back on my feet and make my daughter and family proud of me again.

I finally was hired as a mortgage broker. Within six months, the company already had given me my own branch of the mortgage and wholesaling side of the business. I had about 15 employees and was earning close to $1 million a year.

This was a reminder to me of how I originally succeeded, so I continue to identify the most successful person I can find in whatever new field I try, and always ask that person to mentor me. I have always done extremely well whenever I use that model. I am very blessed and humbled to be able to say I have changed my life; now I look forward to mentoring others on a day-to-day basis.

There are good and bad people out there, and people who are always looking for shortcuts in life, which is what happened to me. At one point in my life, I tried to take a shortcut—and I went to jail. The shortcuts in life will cut the legs right out from underneath you. When you make mistakes in life, you pay a price. What is unfortunate is that when you get out of jail or prison, there are few people who will say, "Let me help you get back on your feet."

If you are trying to get back up after a divorce, or bankruptcy, or even if you went to jail, the only thing that is going to get you out of your current situation is massive action.

That is what I did. I told myself that until I had $1 million in liquid cash in my pocket and a certain amount put away, I would not pay for entertainment—not even a television. With great achievement comes great sacrifice, so if you are out there trying to make things happen, but you come home at 6 p.m. and you put up your feet and decide to eat bonbons and watch

TV the rest of the evening, you are not that motivated. You may *say* you are, but your actions will dictate where you are going to end up.

Everyone should want a mentor; the question is, does everyone *deserve* to have a mentor? Because you ask someone to mentor you does not mean that person will decide to do so. You may have to prove yourself worthy first. What are you doing to show that mentor you deserve to be mentored?

If your mentor tells you that you need to go and do something, don't return and ask for more guidance until you have completed the first set of instructions you received. Your action and your perseverance will be the reason your mentor sees you shine.

Network marketing has created more millionaires than any other industry in the world, but when you talk to people who don't understand it, they believe it is a pyramid scheme. But true network marketing is about leveraging yourself off what other people do. It is no different than the military, the church, or a regular business model.

When I talked to people about getting into network marketing, people advised against it. Friends were not against me succeeding, but they urged caution.

A wise person once told me, "Billy, nothing against your friends or family, but never take advice from somebody who is not earning what you want to be earning." That made a lot of sense to me. Find someone who is successful in that same business or is at the very least successful in something else and ask that person for advice.

I reached out to the most successful person I personally knew at that time in my life, my best friend's husband, Rich Cartagena, and asked for his feedback.

"Billy," Rich said, "I believe if you really want it, have the right people leading you, and have the right products, you can do anything you want. If this is something that you want to take on, I believe you'll be success."

When Rich told me I could do it, I went out and did it—I made it happen. I had great success in network marketing, but about four years ago, I decided it was time to follow my passion back into the medical field and take advantage of my knowledge and my own network. I found the person who was the best at what I was doing and got on the phone with him every chance I had. Within three weeks, I had landed some very large accounts. This proved I still needed mentors; I turned right around and mentored others in turn. I built a network.

Build that network and stay in contact with those you mentor; be true to them. As mentors, it is our obligation to breath belief into the people we are mentoring. Too many mentors fail to do that.

Sometimes people run into hurdles and it is a mentor's job to help them get back on track. Mentors cannot give up on the people they are mentoring. Many people out there lose their vision for a little while and stop moving forward. Often, if they had just kept their foot on the gas, they would have pushed through to the other side and finished the race.

There should be nothing between you and your goals. No matter what comes your way, you should be laser-focused and let nothing stop you.

Once you master that, teach it to others. In a nutshell, your mentorship and network can dictate the outcome of your own success.

Biography

For the last twenty-one years, Billy Womack has brought excellence to the entrepreneurial game. After playing college basketball and serving in the USAF, he became a top sales consultant for a multi-billion-dollar company. He went on to become a sports marketing agent for professional athletes, then owned a nightclub and sushi restaurant.

After detouring into drugs and paying the price by going to jail, he turned his life around again and became a success phenomenon. Today, though he is a seven-figure entrepreneur, he wants to help people understand that their past does not necessarily determine their future. He puts much of his energy into mentoring and teaching others how to break through their mental barriers. Billy plans to release his book, "From Bars to Stars" coming in 2019.

One of his favorite quotes is: *Where we've been has nothing to do with where we're going. We ALL deserve a second chance."*

Billy lives in Tampa, Florida.

Contact Information:

Get Socially Connected
with Billy Womack by visiting
www.BillyWomack360.com

CHAPTER SIX

The Gates of Change

Roxie Nunnally

One day when I was driving down the highway, God took me on a journey that would change my life forever. He called on me to raise my standards.

When God called on me, I reached for Him with these exact words: *Jesus Christ, come on in!* A man had shared these words with me more than twenty years before, when I was a teenager, and remembering these powerful words saved my life forever.

Today I share these powerful words with you. They're the gates of change, the beginning of where your own breakthrough will lead you. Think about that. Is your whole heart in what you are doing? If not, raise the standards of what your life could be. My strength comes from my standards, and I've embraced God's standards for my life.

I have a high calling. I will not live with low standards. I encourage you to set the same standards, standards that are acceptable to our King. We all must take responsibilities for our attitudes. The gates of change starts with our standards.

Embrace the standard of equality. Don't sit in judgment. Don't violate the primary thing which will give us unity. Don't complain. (How can I live in a joyful state if I continue to complain?) Incorporate some meditation into your routine; meditation will change your life and set your mood for each day. It doesn't matter if you choose morning, afternoon, or evening—include 10 minutes of meditation every day.

Growing Up

My dad was very abusive to my mom and he'd be drunk most of the time. One day she decided to leave him for good. His outcome was going to jail; it was all he knew. When we were old enough, we were able to put our names on his visitation list, but I was not interested in going to jail to visit him. No hard feelings, but I was already in a good place with what the Lord above had created for me.

As a single parent, my mom often didn't know how she would feed her six children. I have a lot of respect for her because we all turned out okay. We lived in a one-bedroom shotgun house where she slept in a chair and my siblings and I shared the same bed. She worked in the food service industry, and I finally figured out it was because she could bring us leftover food when things were really tough. God is a provider.

Growing up, I was quiet and shy. My mom always told us that when we go to school to be on our best behavior. She also told us what it would look like if we decided to stray. I believed her. No convincing needed.

Every day students bullied other students and misbehaved in class. This was the norm for our school and our gang-infested neighborhood in the heart of South Memphis. Teachers spent most of their day reprimanding rather than teaching. I didn't appreciate going into class and not being able to learn.

Fast forward to high school.

Boy, did I love Spanish class! No matter what students tried to get away with in class, Señor Weir wasn't going for any of it. He was truly amazing. He talked to us only in Spanish, and his rule was if we wanted anything (to go to the restroom, get a Kleenex, etc.) we had to ask *en español*. No exceptions. We had no choice but to learn Spanish. He's one of the teachers who I have never forgotten, and I would give the world to see him again. Señor Weir was passionate about his occupation, no matter how the students acted out. He just paid them no mind.

Our school sponsored a series of inspirational programs, inviting speakers who had beaten the odds to share their stories with students. One speaker made a big impression on me. She told us she also had grown up in a bad neighborhood, hearing bullet shots every day, yet she knew there was more in life for her than what she was exposed to. Everyone in the auditorium listened. She went on to say, "In life, some people dream, but others never do. In order to become anyone in life that's *good*, you have to start somewhere you've never been. In order to do anything *right*, you must take risks. *It's not where you come* from that determines whether you will be part of the have or have-not groups. If I can just help one person in this room, then I'm successful."

I thought to myself, "I'm not sure how many spots she has, but I know I'm going to be at least *one* of the people she helps." I listened to everything she said and was determined not to look away for a second until she was done.

I got my first job at Liberty Land, a local amusement park, and it allowed me to have a little money in my pocket and help my mom out. My senior year, I got a job at a McDonald's near my house. It was great and horrible at the same time. I remember walking in grease on the floor, sliding around all day and thinking, "Now I know why I should go to college."

In high school, I was no longer shy. Some of the students got a kick out of how I spoke, and they often said, "You talk really funny. Can you please repeat what you just said?"

It made no sense, but I went along with them, sometimes adding emphasis and a little drama in my voice. They would laugh and ask me to repeat, sometimes eight or nine times.

In my senior year, I was asked if I would do the formal welcome speech for an upcoming honor society program. I was a bit confused as to why it wasn't someone from the honor society. *I* sure hadn't been asked to be on the honor society— my grades sucked. (Not until I got to college did I realize the importance of grades and finally make the Dean's list.)

I asked, "Out of all the students in the school, why would you pick me?"

"Before I answer you, I should tell you who our special speaker is going to be."

"Who is it?" (As if I would know the person anyway.)

"Mr. Spike Lee."

I *do* know who he is, I thought to myself, and I certainly know he is famous for making movies—but why is he coming to *our* school? I knew one thing, though: If anyone needs to hear *anything is possible,* the students at my school surely could, including me.

The young lady said, "The students, faculty, and honor society members chose you, and I didn't know why, but after speaking to you, I think that it is pretty obvious, even if your grades aren't the highest. You are the strongest link of us all in this case. Every student they talked to said, 'Let Roxie do it because no one else can fill her shoes much at all.'"

I thought about the many times students asked me to repeat what I said and smiled. I agreed to give the welcome, which I wrote myself. A lot of fun, right? Yes, it *was* fun.

The day finally came and I was sitting directly next to Mr. Lee on the stage. No worries, I knew how to act. I was first on the program, standing tall at the podium in my new white suit. My new white patent leather pumps gave me three additional inches of height. When I finished, there was a standing ovation, and I took a seat, smiling.

Mr. Lee stood up to speak, and yes, it was powerful. I listened to every word he said.

"There is no such thing as an overnight success," he told us.

I took that quote with me everywhere from that moment on. When the program concluded, everyone on stage went backstage with Mr. Lee, including me, as I thought, *You're not leaving **me** behind. This will be my once-in-a-lifetime chance to meet this guy and I am not going to miss out.* I shook his hand very firmly and took some photos with him.

That was the moment I knew I was called to be more than what was just outside my door.

Adulthood

The time came when I graduated from high school. I was the happiest person in the world even though I knew nothing about adulthood.

Most of the girls in my graduation class were pregnant or already had a baby or two. I counted only two girls who weren't with child, and I was one of them. When I went off to college, I lived in a dorm on the campus. I hid from the students who partied 24/7, but I did start dating a musician I met at church. When I learned he wasn't The One, that he had a woman at every church where he played, I wanted out, but not soon enough. I became pregnant and had to leave college in my second semester.

This was not my intention, and it hurt. I knew having a child at 19 and receiving public assistance would not be my final destination. I applied for jobs so I could find a better place for my child and me, and I wanted out of public assistance.

My first adult job was as an assistant manager at Blockbuster, which I enjoyed. After a month, I got a call from my case worker. "I see you've been working."

"That's correct."

"You have a choice to continue receiving benefits or quit your job."

I did the math in my head and I realized that there was no comparison. It was never my goal to stay on public assistance, it was just to help me get on my feet. I told her, "I've only been working for one month; I need more time to get on my feet."

"I can't help you with this."

"I'm not quitting my job to stay on a system that enables people to do nothing more but wait for the limited benefits to come once a month. I'm not going to sit on the porch and wait for food stamps and Aid to Families with Dependent Children."

"Your account has been updated," she said, and she ended the call.

I thought to myself, *I am going to work my behind off to see that I never have to go back to such a system.*

When I was promoted to store manager a year later, I knew the job wasn't my future, even though I enjoyed it, and I would re-enroll in school someday. It took two more years, but I did

THE GATES OF CHANGE

go back to college and start finishing what I had started.

After a brief roller-coaster interlude of dating, I decided to just focus on school and work. A couple of years passed by and I met a guy while I was working in promotion for an NBA team. He walked up and introduced himself, but I really wasn't interested. He wasn't my type. He and I exchanged numbers; when he called, I didn't answer and waited a few weeks before reaching out.

After two years of dating, Avionce and I became engaged. Now he's my husband of more than 15 years, a wonderful man who God sent into my world.

Remember, *he* was the one who *wasn't my type*. Be careful when looking for a certain type of mate. What you get may not look like what you planned.

The biggest breakthrough in my life is when God saved me. I look back over some of my successes and I know it was not because of my work but because of God's work, *period*. It's all about what God orders to happen in your life, and then your breakthrough will manifest itself. God's orders are for us to fulfill our ordained purpose on earth.

In life, it's all about what we go through and retain on our journeys. After all, journeys are meant to be remembered and shared in some capacity or another. I realized we don't care to share some of the bad memories—but think about it—we made it through! That alone can be viewed as a breakthrough.

I want to bless you all with something important: *Remember that people know not what they do.* When someone does something wrong to you, forgive them. Pray for them. Set them free. Give them to God.

When someone calls you and their number isn't in your phone, that means you don't know them. If you're a Christian and you place a call to God, he has your number in his contact list. Some people *say* they're Christians, yet God would never keep their number in his contact list. Beware of false Christians and never lower your standards. If someone does something wrong to you, forgive that person and give them to God, who will bless him.

God wants us to forgive *all* people. God says *He* is our provider. God is the light of the world.

Trust God with all your work and tests. I pray every reader of this book will not only be inspired, but will be delivered from the things that bound them. I ask you to pray this prayer I wrote:

Dear God, thank you for preparing me for all of the things before me, behind me, and ahead of me. I pray for all people, including my enemies.

Help me to reach and teach people who are lost. Help me to reach out to the souls who scream for help but know not where they ought to go. Forgive me of all my sins. Cleanse and fulfill me. Give me bread from heaven. Forgive my generations of their wrong. Help me to pass your tests on earth. God, continue to mold me to meet the army you have equipped me to meet and do your work together. Let us not follow man on earth but let us follow your word through man. Help me to worship you in truth.

Give me the breakthrough I need to make the best of my time here on earth. Give me grace for where I lack understanding. Amen.

I want each of you to have the provision that God intended for us all to have. The provision is here and now. It's always here—and so is the bread. When they put the bread in Jesus' hand, the bread multiplied. There will be enough to go around.

Stay close to Christ *no matter what*. He is the bread of life, and the bread became blessed when it got close to God. You do not have to be good enough; just get near the one who is good enough—*God*. God will supply all of your needs.

Stop wasting today's grace trying to fight tomorrow's battles. Do not be attached to the past. God will do new things in your life.

I want you all to read **Break Through** in its entirety, because your personal breakthrough will continue. Do what God has given you along your journey, good or bad. Do not recreate failure or surround yourself with negative people.

I was meant to share my story and so were you! Think big and you will travel the universe.

Biography

Roxie Nunnally is a serial entrepreneur and a minority business owner and leader. She is a certified spiritual coach, author, a success and motivational speaker and coach, global market analyst, inventor, investor, teacher, and leader. Roxie's known world-wide for her ability to empower business owners to grow their businesses, drawing from her experience owning multiple retail, human resources, media, financial audit and services, legal services, entrepreneurial academy, branding, logistics, and marketing businesses of her own, plus franchises and non-profits. Her grant writing successes are legendary.

Her multiple degrees include a B.B.A.(Business Administration with a concentration in Management), M.B.A. (Master of Business in Administration with a concentration in Human Resource Management), and M.A.T (Master of Arts in Teaching with a concentration in General and Special Education).

Roxie has received many awards and accolades for her community involvement and worldwide affiliations. She serves on her Shelby County and Memphis Equal Opportunity Commissions; Shelby County Division of Corrections In-Reach Board; the Community Emergency Response Team as a member and Instructor; volunteers with the American Red Cross as a CPR/First Aid/AED/pediatrics instructor;

the Tennessee Developmental Disability Council (West TN Region) as a policy maker and partner; is a Public Information Officer for Medical Support Command, City of Memphis; is in the Office of Emergency Management Reserve for the Shelby County Office of Preparedness Reserve; is an Ambassador for the Shelby County Sheriff's Citizen Academy and the Memphis Police Department. Roxie is a member of more leadership and mentor programs than can be included here.

Roxie often speaks to legislators about changing and incorporating new policies. She has great interest in the global marketplace and is fluent in Spanish and conversant in Chinese.

Currently, Roxie is President of 4D Marketing & Business Solutions Firm Corp, a worldwide marketing and branding firm, and is founder and overseer of Lewis Help Today Foundation, a 501(c) (3) organization.

Roxie and her husband, Avionce, have three children and live in Memphis, Tennessee, Dallas, Texas, and Los Angeles, California.

Contact information

Email: Z4dmarketing.biz.rn@outlook.com
Website: www.4dmarketingbusinesssolutions.com
Facebook: www.facebook.com/RoxieNunnally/

CHAPTER SEVEN

Anxiety Can Affect Anyone

Phillip "Paris Lazarus" Bilal

It was the summer of 2016 and I was only 18, had just graduated from high school, signed my first record deal, was working with Grammy-nominated producers, and I even had been cosigned by hip hop legend Yung Joc. On the outside, my life was perfect. Incredible, even.

Inside me, though, things were very dark. I was having a huge internal battle, and despite my success, I had no confidence in myself. I was in a toxic relationship, I lost someone who was a father figure to me, and I self-medicated. Though I was struggling with many mental health issues, the most prominent one in my life, one I still live with today, is anxiety.

The Merriam-Webster dictionary defines anxiety as "an abnormal and overwhelming sense of apprehension and fear often marked by physical signs (such as tension, sweating, and increased pulse rate), by doubt concerning the reality and nature of the threat, and by self-doubt about one's capacity to cope with it."

I sure can vouch for that. I could have written the definition myself.

Instead, I'm writing this chapter to help those who struggle with anxiety daily. I promise you, regardless of money, status, or fame, anxiety can affect *anyone*.

We all enjoy spending time with loved ones and friends, and they are the people with whom we usually feel the most comfortable. I never thought I would discover my anxiety while I was chilling in a hot tub with my best friends. It was a beautiful sunny day in Los Angeles, and I'd invited my friends over to workout and relax at the spa. After the workout, we all headed to the hot tub to relax, and suddenly I felt an overwhelming feeling of unease and panic.

Here I was joking and laughing with my friends, but my heart was racing inside me, almost like my body was telling me that I was in fight or flight mode. I had experienced this feeling before but had no idea what it was or what it meant. I mean, seriously, I was in one of the most relaxing situations possible, yet I didn't feel remotely relaxed.

Soon, I started experiencing aggressive insomnia and began waking up from a deep sleep in a total panic. My lack of sleep became so overwhelming that I knew I had to do something about it. When I told my mom, she scheduled a doctor's appointment immediately. After asking me a series of personal questions, it didn't take long for my doctor to diagnose me with general anxiety disorder. I always had a feeling something was wrong, even though I was experiencing a lot of success. The doctor offered up a variety of solutions including sleep medication, therapy, and exercise. My mom and I discussed the options the doctor offered, and we both came to the conclusion that I shouldn't rely on sleep medication.

After my diagnosis, I tried to come to terms with why I had anxiety. There had to be some clear cause for the condition.

Though I've had many father figures growing up, my Uncle Sean was the true definition of a man. My mother and I met him shortly after moving to Los Angeles from Houston. He was kind, charismatic, and he took me under his wing to teach me important life lessons. Over the years, our bond grew stronger and stronger, and he was always there for me at my lowest moments. Uncle Sean was a prestigious basketball coach in the community and he made sure every kid felt special whether they were a good player or not. He pushed us all toward excellence and never gave up on any of us. He truly was a stand-up guy and his lessons and memory have shaped me into the young man I am today.

I remember this like it was yesterday: I'd just warmed up on my trumpet for my final high school band concert. As I was scrolling through Twitter to check on a basketball game, my heart dropped; Uncle Sean had just passed away from a heart attack. I was devastated, and it was so bad I honestly didn't know how to react. I started receiving calls and text messages from old teammates who were just as shocked as I was. While I did cry, I knew I had an important performance and he would've wanted me to push through and nail it.

Internally, I really hurt; however, I pushed the grief away because it was my senior year and I was trying not to end it on a sour note. During my senior year I had finally became popular at school and was having the time of my life. For most of my high school experience, I never really fit in, but it had all changed that year. Ironically, it was my uncle's advice that led me to join the school band and eventually the football team because he wanted me to be more social.

I ran away from the pain and sorrow because I wanted to enjoy my last months with some of my best friends. To cope with his death, I smoked weed and drank alcohol regularly, and I partied every chance I could to hopefully distract myself, even if it was temporary. While I thought it would help at the time, this clearly wasn't healthy. Uncle Sean was the person I looked up to and trusted with my life, and I tried too hard to stay strong when I should've been grieving properly. Looking back at that time, this was definitely a contributing factor to my anxiety.

Love is an amazing thing, but it also can be very damaging and addictive. I think most people have all had a "first" love before. You know, that one person who you can never forget, no matter how many people you date afterward. I met my first love during my junior year. Michele was extroverted, confident, and extremely charming—pretty much my exact opposite. I'm an introvert almost to the most extreme, however, most of my friends will tell you that once you get to know me I'm an open book.

When I met the girl who was my first love, I had recently moved from another school. I had a hard time fitting in because I was one of the only black kids at the school and the kids who did try to be friendly to me seemed superficial and insincere. Michele was always different, though; she never seemed to follow the crowd and always believed in her own ideas—which she and I had in common.

She was more than just a person I dated. Beyond the romantic relationship, we were truly best friends. We understood each other, and I'd never met another person I could talk to for hours and hours and never get bored. We just clicked. From the first time we dated, I was truly in love with Michele. She made me feel safe, she made me feel like I could tell her anything without worrying about her giving out my secrets. While we did have our issues, no matter what happened, our friendship brought us back together.

The summer before my senior year, I planned on joining the football team and I was super excited about taking Michele to prom. When she said her parents invited me to join them on a road trip to a mountain resort for the Fourth of July, my mom said it was okay and I happily joined them. This was big for me; her parents' invitation meant that they must've thought highly of me. Michele and I had a blast. I had never really been to the mountains before and we did so many things while we were up there. We swam in the lake, played at an arcade, walked outside, enjoyed what Mother Nature had in store for us, and most importantly, we watched the beautiful fireworks.

When the trip was over, I felt amazing and was looking forward to all the memories Michele and I would make together in our senior year. I was heartbroken when only a few days later she said she didn't want to be with me anymore and thought it was best that we break up.

I'd never felt this way about another person before, and the thought of not being with Michele for the last year of high school devastated me. We didn't talk my whole senior year. I knew she was dating other people and I didn't know how to cope with the pain. My whole year wasn't *too* bad because I made a lot of amazing memories with great people during my senior year, but I missed her and really wanted to talk with her again. It was tough.

Michele tried to reach out multiple times to mend our friendship at the very least, but it was too painful for me, and I felt anxious every time we were in the same room.

High school finally ended, and my friends and I were looking forward to the future. That summer, Michele texted me, asking if we could meet up. She said she would be leaving the country soon and that she really missed me. I decided to meet her and it was great. Hanging out again reminded me why we were so close in the first place. We started meeting up regularly and soon started dating again, even though she kept telling me not to get too attached because she would be leaving soon and she didn't want to hurt me a second time. Of course, following my heart and not my brain, I fell hard for her again.

This time she "ghosted" me—not even giving me the respect of telling me she didn't want to be with me—she just didn't talk to me at all.

The first time we broke up was hard, but this time, it truly broke me. My anxiety was at an all-time high, as I was constantly wondering "why me?" Why wouldn't she love me back? Why wouldn't she at least give me the respect of knowing why she didn't want to be with me? That, combined with my uncle's death, led me to become depressed, suicidal, and anxious almost 24/7.

In my mind, this was my first step to becoming dependent on Xanax.

Los Angeles is known for many things—the beaches, the weather, the women, and, of course, the drugs. But it wasn't until I actually lived there that I understood just how much drugs were a part of Los Angeles culture. By that point, I was signed to a record deal and doing a lot of press and performances. Though this life was what I dreamed of as a kid, I was unhappy. I was in so much internal pain from everything that happened to me in this short span of time.

I was lost and I didn't know what to do. My anxiety was

causing me a lot of trouble, though it hadn't officially been diagnosed. An old friend of mine suggested I try a drug called Xanax. He told me I shouldn't take too much but it would definitely help with my anxiety. I didn't heed his warning and I started taking two a day to help ease my pain.

My dependence on Xanax and its effects on my mental health were really taking a toll on my personal life. My friends started to notice I didn't hang out with them as much as I used to, and when I did, I was generally depressed and quiet. I hardly went outside and stayed in my room all day playing video games or taking an unhealthy amount of naps. I still hadn't grieved the loss of my uncle, and I was still heartbroken over my ex.

I remember the day I reached my breaking point like it was yesterday. It was an overcast day, nothing really special. My friends invited me over to play video games and hang out, but I declined. Instead, I stayed home, took my daily dose of Xanax, and spent most of the day being depressed and taking naps. Suddenly, I decided to go up to my complex's roof and look at the view. I thought it would make me feel better because this roof was where I used to play, smoke, and talk with my friends, and I'd made many memories on this roof that I cherished.

My trip down memory lane turned dark as I looked at the view and thought, "Maybe this is where I end it all." I was so tired of being depressed, anxious, and heartbroken. For an hour, I sat near the edge of my roof, considering if this was meant to be *my* end.

Instead, I decided it was time for me to fight my problems. I got off that roof and told myself, "I'm going to make it no matter what. I won't let my demons defeat me. It's time to love myself."

While it's been a long four years since that moment, I can confidently say I've made my breakthrough.

I bet you're wondering, "So, how *did* you make your breakthrough?"

First off, I decided to make the tough decision of focusing on myself for two months. I loved my friends dearly, but at the time I was not the best version of myself and I needed to start loving myself. I also decided to limit my smartphone use because I realized that using my phone and constantly being worried about other people's lives and how many likes I was getting was making me even more anxious and insecure.

When I started looking into ways to ease my anxiety, I found an enormous number of articles about meditation as a great way to ease anxiety. I meditated daily from that day forward and became less anxious day by day. For those of us dealing with anxiety, meditation is a great way to begin the day and ease our mind. Meditation allows us to have time for ourselves, which is hard to do these days because most of us are always on the move. More importantly, it's a perfect way to truly get to know yourself and become more self-aware.

As I started working out and adding even more healthy habits, I found a feature on my smart phone that allowed me to limit my social media time. Most people in my generation view working out as boring; however, working out daily for about 30 minutes can really help us all reduce stress and even improve self-confidence. Working out helped me immensely because it gave me a daily goal and it made me feel way more confident in myself.

The last part of my breakthrough was finding my true purpose. Our world is extremely chaotic and confusing, which makes people question, "What is the point of it all?" There truly is no single right answer, but finding what you really want to do with your life will give you more motivation to push through your mental issues. From a very young age, I knew I loved music and loved writing. Fortunately, I'm talented in both areas, so I've set my goals on becoming a platinum-selling artist and a best-selling author. These days, I'm much more ambitious and driven. I evolve every day, step by step, and it's been so satisfying to feel my growth.

For all of you out there who deal with anxiety, I want you to know you are unique, strong, and deserve to be here. Two years ago, I was unsure if I even wanted to live anymore; now I'm part of this amazing book, and hopefully will help inspire all of you to go out there and follow your dreams.

As you make your own breakthrough, remember your past does not define you, and you can do *anything* if you follow your heart, remain humble, and work hard.

Biography

Born in New York City and raised in Houston, Texas, Phillip Bilal has always perfectly filled the definition of "a creative." Known widely as Paris Lazarus, the award-winning musician, podcast producer, writer, and YouTube star has co-written his first book.

His chapter in *Break Through* delves into his struggles with mental health disorders, the most prominent being crippling anxiety. Phillip offers an inside view of what it's like to struggle with mental health issues, and he lays out the steps he took to make a breakthrough to a better mindset.

Phillip currently resides in Houston and is pursuing his college degree while finding time to also focus on his passions.

Contact Information

Email: parislazarus@gmail.com
Facebook: Paris Lazarus
Twitter: @Parislazarus
Instagram: @Parislazarus
YouTube: Paris Lazarus

CHAPTER EIGHT

All That Matters
Is You

Natalie Masset

You could say the year 2018 was very challenging for me: I almost died three times. That's a lot of challenge for any year—even if it *was* the year I turned 30.

I was born in Prague, the capital city of what is now known as the Czech Republic. The country was influenced by the 40-year political separation from the West, but as I was born, the political situation was changing and big things were starting to happen in our country.

My family had roots in France and we were very interested in culture and literature. Though everyone in my family had university degrees, we were five people living in a modest rented apartment—my grandmother, my parents, my brother, and me. We didn't have a lot of money because my mother was an invalid and could no longer work, but my parents always loved each other and took care of us. Even as a child, I realized how much my father worked and how hard it was for us to be able to live as well as we did. They were often so tired, and I wondered, *Why is it like that?*

When I was a child, I was very curious and always wanted

to know why things happened. That´s also the reason I was not happy at school; people didn't appreciate my curiosity. I loved reading and learning, but I hated the school system and the way we learned—the drill.

As I grew older, I learned there were people more tired than my father and my mother—people who were really poor and didn't have a nice life at all. I came to realize the answer was our country's bad education system, which did not support the development of personality. When children are in an education system such as the Czech system that forces them to be average and prohibits independent thinking, they'll never reach their adult potential.

In those school systems, children always hear negative words and phrases such as *never, ever; you can´t; you might not; you should not; and you must not.* They don't often hear positive words and phrases like *try it again; yes, you can; if you really want,* and *you can!* When children repeatedly hear negative words from their own parents, neighbors, teachers, and others who affect them, they start believing they are supposed to be average and just do what someone tells them.

That is the reason why I left my country; I believed I could find a better life living in a free Western country. When I graduated and decided to go to Germany, I was 19 and I couldn´t speak any German. My family's reaction was complicated; not really bad, but my mother, especially, was afraid for me.

My classmates also were not supportive.

"Are you really so naive to think people are waiting there in the Western countries for someone like *you*?" one asked me with a cheeky smile.

"I truly believe there *are* people there waiting for someone like me," I said with conviction.

As he laughed at me and my naiveté, other classmates told me no one from the East could ever get anything better than a cleaning job in any Western country. Many friends warned me I might be sold as a sex slave or killed, with my organs sold to rich people. I was not afraid. I was so excited that it was impossible to feel any fear.

"I'm not going to live my life imprisoned in a system in which I don´t believe," I said, while telling them about Madeleine Albright and other famous Czechs who left the country and have done well.

The truth is I didn´t want to be the next famous someone—I wanted to be *me*, a happy me. I just didn´t know what kind of me or what kind of someone I would like to become. I only knew I had to go and find it by myself.

Something in me was burning and pushing me forward; I just had to do it, find it, discover it, and live it.

I just wanted to *go*.

I arrived in Germany with one bag, barely any money, and with no knowledge of German, which prevented me from getting a job. I used all the money I had to attend German language courses, every day Monday to Friday, 8 a.m. to 2 p.m. I traveled by foot, saving my money for class supplies. Even if it was raining, even if it was snowing, even if I was sick—*no matter what*—every day I walked through the city as if it was a sunny summer day. Step by step, day by day.

One day, social workers came to our classroom and asked us if we wanted some kind of part-time job. I said I needed any job that I could do after school, and got a job helping in a restaurant kitchen.

If my Czech classmates had seen me, they would have laughed, "Now you have reached your dreams in the west."

But I was very happy to get that job. I earned enough money to continue with the school and sometimes visit other cities around me. I was living in the cellar of an older building, and the bath and toilet for everyone living there was on the first floor. My room had everything I needed—a heater, bed, chair, table, wardrobe, and electric light. I didn't need anything more; I just focused on important things.

Every night while I rested on my hard bed I thought about my day and how much I had learned, about the day I would have tomorrow, and about the things I would like to do and see and feel in the future. Afterward, I fell asleep happily. I knew it was only a hard period in my life and soon my better lifetime would come. At the end of the year, I passed my exams with the best grades in my class. I was pleased and decided to continue studying.

The language certificate gave me better jobs and now I could afford trips to neighboring countries. During one trip, I met my future husband, Patrick Masset. He was born into a farming family in France, and as he laughingly reminds us, his small village had more cows than people. His parents made everything they needed; milk, cheese, and meat came from their cows, they grew vegetables and fruit, and they made homemade bread. Even though his parents couldn't help him financially, he earned his bachelor and master's degrees, his doctorate, and later his professorship.

Though he came from an average farm family in the middle of the French Alps, he changed his life, made his dreams come true, and became a scientist. I felt he was like me. The same personality. The same mentality. Just a person making his dreams come true.

We married when I was 21, and we moved to the former East Germany because a university in East Germany offered great scientific projects for my husband's career. I thought about what I wanted to do in my life and what I should study. I always wanted to have a big family and I wanted to hold a job while raising a family. I believe the only way to live happily with a good life and make the world a better place is through learning and developing, so I decided to become a teacher. I chose pre-school education at one university and social education at another, passed both entrance exams, and was accepted to both schools. After finishing the first semester at both schools to see which one I liked more, I found each so interesting that I continued attending both.

I loved what and how we were learning at the university—there was no drill and we had the freedom to learn. The approach made sense to me; I felt it was how it should be. We were there to learn how to *learn*, and later, to teach. After my first year at both universities, I knew I had two more years to get my diplomas.

I'd always known I'd like to have a large family, and I was ready to start it. Many friends told me not to have children until I finished the university, but I didn't listen to them. I was 22 years old when Pierre, our first son, was born. Everybody thought he would end my studies, but I believe having children doesn't mean life should stop, so I continued studying at both universities until I graduated. Life was going well, so I decided to continue studying for one more year to get a certificate for adult education. When I was 25, our second son, Antoine, was born, and I finished at my third university.

I wanted to become a great teacher, change the world around me, and make it a better place. When I started to work as a teacher, though, I was not happy—not at the first school where I taught, and not anywhere else, either. I tried other schools, and realized the reality was very different from what we studied. The students had no connection between the subjects and deep understanding.

Though I knew I had invested many years in studying, I didn't want to support a system in which I didn't believe. My husband reached the same point. He was educating university students, and he realized most were not interested in deep understanding, just in preparing themselves for exams and forgetting what they learned as quickly as possible. We agreed our students were 90% well-educated sheep and 10% free-minded personalities.

We had such a stressful life. We were "successful" and "rich" by many people's standards, but we were not happy. We almost didn't have time to see each other; we had no time to breathe. We had money but no time to spend it. This was just destroying us, so we both decided to make changes. We quit our jobs and decided to start again from the beginning, being independent and helping each other to become independent. We became entrepreneurs, working only with other entrepreneurs. This was the only thing that made sense.

If I can make this change, and if my husband can, so can everybody else, too. We are nothing special, I am not more intelligent or better than anybody else. I just asked myself, *Is this the life I want to have? Is this everything? Do I want to live like this for the next 40 years?* I wanted *more.* We both wanted more! We both knew the only limits we faced were in our minds.

When we decided to open our company, it was not easy. Our two daughters, Mariella and Annabelle, had already been born and we had a lot of overhead. It was a year before we started to earn money, and we used all of our savings and took out a loan to survive.

The next two years were better. The company was earning money and we were happy in our private and professional life. We could do a lot of things with our four children; we went on holidays, and I had time to educate them in four languages and do activities as a family.

In January 2018, I had the entire year planned. I wanted to travel in more countries. I wanted to send my oldest son to horse camp and take the children to France for a month to visit their grandparents. I wanted the children to take an art course and continue with the language school . . . and . . . there was a long list of wishes.

I always have wishes and dreams and I make them come true. But this year was different. I didn´t know my life would change. One day in January, my husband was out with our oldest and I was at home with our three other children. Suddenly, I felt a terrible pain in my back. I had never felt a pain like that before. I thought maybe I moved wrong and maybe it was nothing. Then I felt so terrible, I had to lie down on my bed. Within ten minutes my body was shaking uncontrollably and I almost couldn´t move. With my last energy, I called my husband.

That probably saved my life. My husband took me to the hospital and they did immediate surgery. My right kidney had stopped working. Two months later, the second kidney also stopped functioning. In total, I had five surgeries within four months. During that time, I couldn´t do anything, just lay on the bed. I was in so much pain, I almost couldn´t move. It was a big challenge to go to the bathroom, and I definitely couldn't care for my children.

This was the worst period in my life. I was in bed, looking out the window every day at the sun shining in the sky, and thinking about how to manage the situation. I knew I was not yet 30 years old and I had almost died twice. I knew all our plans for 2018 were gone, and the situation was bad.

I decided to use my time and study as much as I could. I read a lot of books to encourage myself, master the pain, and recover. April 29 was the last day I was ill. My doctor told me I could slowly start doing things again, but I would have to follow a special kidney diet my whole life because there is a high risk of relapse.

The next day, I told my children I'd be gone for a little while, and texted the friend I was about to meet, "See you soon." I drove to the town near our home but never arrived. The only thing I can remember is a car driving into the front of my car. I learned the crash pushed my car off the road and I was trapped inside. People who saw the accident got me out and called the ambulance. I received a very serious concussion, and still have health complications.

I think about everything that happened to me this year. Everything that happens in life is for a reason, and sometimes we don´t see the reason immediately. My life changed. My whole family's life changed. If we were not entrepreneurs, probably we would be financially ruined. But even now, I truly believe better days are coming. I always have believed it.

I have choices. I could see 2018 as a tragedy: *My health was ruined, our plans for 2018 destroyed, and I might never be able to drive again.* I could also see it in a different way: *I'm thankful for everything I have. I survived kidney disease and a bad car accident. Even though I have health problems, I'm not in a wheelchair. Even though I cannot do everything as before, my family, friends, a housekeeper, and a doctor help me.*

What I would like to say to everyone who reads my story is this:

It doesn't matter where you come from or if you are a man or woman. Your native language, your color or religion, your economic status, how many children you have, and if you sit in a wheelchair or lie in bed *also* do not matter. The only thing that matters is *you* and the way you think about life and its challenges.

The people with the hardest lives often can accomplish the most. Steven Hawking was paralyzed and in a wheelchair but he was one of the greatest physicists in history. J.K. Rowling was in a dire financial situation when she wrote the first Harry Potter book and she became a multi-millionaire. Steve Jobs started Apple in primitive conditions in his garage and he built the wealthiest and most famous company in the world.

There are many others I could write about—people who had passion for what they did and loved their work. I believe every person has a talent—it is only necessary to discover it. Everyone can become successful and have a better life.

In my case, I decided to become the best person I can be and help as many people as I can be healthy and happy and have enough to eat, enough fresh water, enough clothes, and a place to live. For everyone who has those things already, I want to help them find their talents and find a way to fulfillment. This is the best gift I can give as a teacher and the reason why I studied—to support real people and help them have a chance to change their lives.

I know I can do it. I deeply believe it's possible to change lives and the world independently of whether I am healthy or not. Ten years ago, I didn´t speak a word of German. Ten years ago, I was alone, living in a cellar. This year I almost died— three times! A few months ago, I couldn't get out of bed. And today, I live with my husband and four children in our nice home and I am co-writing a book with Johnny Wimbrey, Les Brown, and Nik Halik.

Can you imagine what I was thinking about ten years ago? Ten years ago, I knew I would have a better future, but I couldn´t imagine my reality now. This only proves nothing is impossible and everything is possible! *For everyone*.

Johnny Wimbrey´s life, Les Brown´s life, Nik Halik´s life, and the lives of the other authors in this book show that if you *really* want to do so, you can change your life forever.

I know there are millions of people who want more from life, and they are ready to do something to change their lives. They just have to know about the possibilities and how to get what they want. I would like to tell them how and why I did it. I would like to show them that this is possible for them. Everything is possible for every woman and man in the world.

I am 30 years old, I have four children, and I am still alive after all that happened this year. The breakthrough. I got it! Other people can get it, too.

Let´s tell them about it!

Biography

Natalie Masset is an educator in preschool, social education, and adult learning, as well as a transformation teacher, life coach, trainer and motivational speaker. Her main focus lies in personal development and life fulfillment. She especially helps people to combine their private and professional lives, which she's successfully done as an entrepreneur and the mother of four young children.

Natalie and her husband founded **Lifestyleacademy24**, where coaching and inspiration programs are offered and where participants can learn and prove their business knowledge and skills. This project also works as a community platform for new business opportunities for young entrepreneurs.

Contact Information:

www.nataliemasset.com
Facebook: Natalie Masset
Instagram: Lifestyleacademy24

CHAPTER NINE

Fulfill Your Purpose

Raison Thompson

What makes you so special? What makes you unique or sets you apart from the rest of the more than seven billion souls in the world? Answering those questions is the first step toward discovering our purpose—the most important truth about our existence in the universe. Purpose gives validation and justification for something's existence. Purpose is the "why?" of a thing. Purpose literally justifies an individual's life on this planet and even the planet itself.

We must distinguish the difference between function and purpose because even though the two terms seem similar in definition, their meanings are vastly different. A bulldozer and a shovel both have the same function—they both dig holes. However, both have unique and drastically different purposes. When an inventor created the first shovel, he needed to create a small hole in the ground, so the tool's design accommodates gardeners with that need. The creator of the bulldozer began with the needs of construction crews who had to dig and move large quantities of earth to lay the foundations for buildings or roads.

In each case, the tool's purpose determined every significant aspect of its existence. Purpose determined its design, the cost of production, the type of person who would be using it, and the industry that it would be used in. Ultimately, purpose sheds light on the most compelling aspect of each tool—each one has a creator.

Purpose proves all things were created and didn't happen by accident because their creator gave each thing its purpose. All human beings on this planet have a purpose for their lives, and the origin of our individual purpose is in the heart and mind of our Creator.

By virtue of this truth, we can find comfort in knowing we were designed deliberately. There was an intent behind the creation of every one of us. The creators of the bulldozer and shovel derived their purpose from a need or a set of needs. Likewise, your Creator designed you to solve or meet a set of needs. You were created to solve a problem and your true fulfillment in life will begin the moment you identify your life's purpose.

I believe my perspective makes me unique from the other seven billion people on this planet, and it's one of the aspects of my life I can duplicate in the lives of others through teaching and affect positive change in the world. Why perspective? Because I interpret perspective as "the way that one perceives a situation." I have discovered perspective is indeed a powerful asset, especially in times of adversity, confusion, and disappointment. An individual's circumstances can be completely against them, but *how*, *when*, and *where* they look at their situation will ultimately determine their response, thus determining the outcome.

Perspective is a component of an individual's mindset, and mindsets can be difficult to change. So how do you transform a person's perspective? How do you transform the way an individual interprets adversity? Why is it that two people can experience the exact same set of adverse circumstances, and one sees loss while the other sees opportunity?

Your perspective can also be interpreted as your point of view or what you see based on your current position. That is true for both your physical proximity to an object as well as your mental perception of a situation. In both contexts, the principles are the same.

If you place your hand directly in front of your face to the point where your hand touches your nose, you will not be able to see anything except your hand. When you slowly move your hand away, gradually you begin to see more, and eventually you will be able to see the entire world surrounding your hand. As you continue to move your hand away from your face, you will soon realize your hand is very small in comparison to the world around it—you literally see a "bigger picture."

Now imagine that the cares of your life (bills, career, family, relationships, etc.) become your hand, the hand that literally blocks your view. When we experience trouble in our lives or suffer trauma, all we can see is that trouble or trauma. Having a healthy perspective empowers you to see the bigger picture. When you have a healthy perspective, you can see your problem (the one so enormous it's all you can see) is really a very small issue. It's just so close that it blocked your view.

When I was young, I spent a summer living with my grandparents. They lived on a farm in Mississippi, and they ate what they grew. Well, as a child from the suburbs, I wanted to go to McDonald's. I didn't want to eat things like black-eyed peas. When my grandmother prepared dinner for me, I threw a tantrum and shook my head, protesting what was on my plate. My grandmother never became offended. She smiled lovingly, looked at me over the top of her glasses, and said, "You just ain't hungry enough, baby. It will be here when you are ready."

My grandmother was telling me I just hadn't acquired a taste for those black-eyed peas yet. I soon discovered a person can acquire or "develop" an appetite for a particular menu item when given the proper motivation. Needless to say, I learned to like those black-eyed peas. Eventually, I fell in love with them!

There is an ancient Jewish legend about how the Queen of Sheba tested the wisdom of King Solomon by asking him to find the only real bouquet of flowers in a room filled with fakes.

King Solomon accepted the Queen's challenge to figure out at a glance which bouquet was real. After several minutes of sitting motionless, staring at the roomful of beautiful fakes, King Solomon figured out how to find the bouquet of real flowers. He gestured for his servants to open a window, then waited patiently until a bumblebee entered the room and landed on the only real flowers.

In a room full of specially crafted fakes, how did King Solomon know that a simple bumblebee would manage to figure out which bouquet was the real one? The answer is simple—the bee's *appetite* made that possible. Your *appetite* determines what your senses, will, discipline, and resources will be channeled toward. Your *appetite* is the breeding ground for the forces that drive you and influence your impulses and instincts.

Over time, I've developed an appetite for greatness and excellence, so my perspective is always geared to be solution-oriented, rather than disadvantage-oriented. If I had to identify what the breakthrough was in my own life, I couldn't narrow it down to only one event. During my life, I have experienced a series of breakthroughs with each achievement preparing me for the next.

When I was in the fifth grade, I experienced one of the first of many breakthrough moments in my life. All of my friends were playing Pee-Wee Football while I was at home reading books. I noticed that on Saturday mornings, when I went out to play, all of my friends were at the stadium on the football field. I soon felt the urge to go out for one of the local teams.

I remember signing up to play and being so excited about just being out there with my friends, sharing the same experiences. I was a football player!

One by one, we were being measured and weighed by the various coaches. I remember standing in line, high-fiving my friends, as we waited to hear our names called announcing what team we would be on.

After learning of their team selections and receiving their schedules, the rest of the players had gone home for the day. The next thing I knew, I heard a whistle blow and a group of coaches hustled toward those of us who remained with a look of concern that made me feel terribly uneasy.

As we sat on the grass, the president of the league informed each of us that we did not meet the height, weight, or some other physical requirement to play in that league. As for me, he said I exceeded the weight limit for my age group by ten pounds. I remember how hearing those words made me feel numb all over, and I couldn't seem to hear anything after that moment.

Walking back to the car felt like it took forever. The entire time, all I could think of was how my friends were going to laugh at me for being overweight. Sitting in the car, I just stared out the window feeling rejected and inadequate. I felt like a loser. I remember thinking that I never cared about my weight before. In my mind, my friends and I were all the same. But that day, I realized that we weren't. I sobbed all the way home, too ashamed to even look my father in his face.

As we made our way up the driveway to our house, my father said very gently, yet very sternly, "The coach said the first practice is in two weeks. If you can make the weight within that time, you will have a spot on the team." Suddenly, I was ready to celebrate! That was the best news that I had heard all day. I stepped out of the car ready to run through the front door to tell my mom the good news when my father said abruptly, "Not so fast."

I was confused. I couldn't understand why he didn't seem to share in my enthusiasm. But he had other plans. As we stood there, face to face in the driveway, my father tells me, "We have two whole weeks to make weight for the squad. You must drop ten pounds in under fourteen days. That's not a lot of time at all, but you can reach your goal if you don't half-commit. Do you understand?"

"Yes, sir!"

"Four times around the block is a little over a mile," he told me. "I want you to give me four laps around the block with your pads on right now."

That didn't sound like support to me. It sounded like punishment. It felt like my father wasn't interested in me reaching my goals at all. But I took off around the block anyway because I wanted to prove something to myself. When I finished my fourth lap, I thought I was going to pass out, so you can imagine the utter dismay I felt when my father was waiting for me on the front porch with a pitcher of ice water and a beach towel.

"Pop, what is that for?" I asked.

"Your workout isn't over yet," he replied.

I felt my eyes watering with disappointment, but I didn't want to let my father down—and somehow, I didn't want to let myself down. So, I drank up my water and I said, "What's next?"

My father told me to run ten wind sprints in my front yard. By this time, the sun was going down and it was getting dark, so he started the car and turned on the headlights so I could see as I ran my ten sprints.

After about the third wind sprint, I stopped and screamed to my father, "I can't run anymore! My body hurts! You want too much from me!" Then my father taught me a principle that has remained with me to this day. He told me that my body will do whatever my mind tells it to do. So my conditioning literally was for my "mind."

Over time, I realized my father was getting my mind in shape—not just my body. My father knew that a well-conditioned mind has complete dominion over the physical body. However, on the journey to mental dominance, the body will use pain and fatigue to resist what the mind is attempting to impose.

Traditionally we are conditioned to interpret physical pain as a signal that something is wrong. Usually, we respond by complying to the body's desire to stop. But when the mind overrides the body's insistence and asserts its will on the body, eventually, the body will capitulate to the will of the mind.

So, I pushed past the pain and fatigue I was feeling that night and completed my workout. And I completed that workout every night for two straight weeks. My dad and I returned to the league to see if I qualified to play in my age group, and I did.

Because of the lessons he taught me, that same year I was able to help our team win the championship, and I made the all-star team.

By the time I turned ten years old, I learned several principles that became a part of the core of who I am. I learned that pain is nothing more than a feeling. Pain is no different than happiness, fear, or anger, all of which are just feelings. My experience of training with my dad taught me about prioritization.

There are so many people who set goals and never reach them because they prioritize their feelings over their purpose. Both your purpose and your feelings carry within them motives and objectives, and whichever you value more is going to be the motive that governs your life's decisions. In other words, if your feelings are more important to you than your purpose, then you will always ultimately succumb to the motivation of your feelings and never fully reach your goals in life or fulfill your purpose.

Remember, the flip side brings you good news: *If your purpose is more important to you than your feelings, you will **always** be able to override what you feel in order to fulfill that purpose and accomplish your goals.*

Biography

Raison Thompson is one of the most creative, uniquely-gifted talents in the entertainment industry today. He is a gifted rapper, singer, and songwriter. His music has been performed by many soloists, music groups, and choirs, including the Mississippi Chapter of the Gospel Music Workshop of America.

As a rapper, he has worked with legendary recording artist Fred Hammond, and is featured on the album, *Uncle Fred—Texture of A Man*, which peaked at Number Six on Billboard's Top Gospel Albums of 2018.

Raison is an extremely versatile actor who can portray a full range of character types. He has appeared in more than 20 stage productions, feature films like *Carter High*, and commercials for Pepsi and the Dallas Cowboys.

Raison is known for his large physical stature, stage presence, vast range, and his ability to breathe life into characters that have intense personal conflict.

He is an ordained minister who founded several ministries from Mississippi to Texas. He is also the author of the books, *They Shall Be Called the Sons of God* and *The Masculine God*.

Born in Biloxi, Mississippi, Raison's early years were less than glamorous, but with hard work and unmatched discipline, he broke the bonds of mediocrity. Raison graduated from Moss Point High School with Honors while lettering in track, football, and basketball.

After declining multiple offers to focus on sports, Thompson decided to follow his heart and attended Alcorn State University where he received a BS degree in Computer Science & Applied Mathematics.

Raison can be booked for speaking engagements, church services, choir workshops, or seminars,

Contact Information

Email: raisonthompsonbusiness@gmail.com
Facebook: theofficialraisonthompson
Twitter: @RaisonThompson
Instagram: @raisonthompsonofficial

CHAPTER TEN

Confessions

Jacques Sadler

"*Jacques, there is absolutely nothing I can do for you. You have all the tools you need and you just have to get back out there and make it happen. You just have to swing the bat.*"

Those were the words I heard at the end of a two-hour call from someone I saw as a friend and a mentor. You would think that would be all the encouragement I needed to get out and make it happen, but I had never felt more despondent and defeated. As I hung up the phone, I heard those words as nails in my coffin. I had been positive that this man, my friend that I'd known for more than 16 years, was going to help me, no questions asked.

No, it was not the case at all.

That call was three years ago. The memory that sticks in my mind was looking up at the ceiling from my hospital bed, thinking, "Had he just said yes, had he just understood the importance of helping me and how that will change my life, he could save me from all the things that plague me. That would be life changing."

But instead of helping, he told me I had to help myself.

Did I blame him? Absolutely not! Did it make me wonder what my life could have/would have been? Yes! Did it make me question his loyalty as a friend or a mentor? No.

I was always taught a mentor does not choose you—you choose a mentor because you respect that person. A mentor projects an enviable lifestyle. When a mentor corrects you, you don't take offense to it, you take it as a billion-dollar training moment.

Did I question him? No.

Our exchange did make me question myself at that very moment. Who was *I* and what was my character? Was I not good enough, not smart enough? Did I not possess the mental tools to be coached? Do I talk too much or not enough? Did I do something to offend him?

I asked myself hundreds of questions as they led me down the path of self-pity, fear, and doubt.

I wondered why this was happening to me. I didn't ask for this! God would not be punishing me for things I'd done in my past; I thought all was forgiven. *Right?*

I've tried to spend my adult years doing things the right way. I've never hurt or mistreated anyone purposefully and I have made a lot of stupid mistakes that have hurt me alone. So please explain to me how I can be diagnosed with not one but two uncurable illnesses that I cannot control.

No one in my family has had either illness, so neither one is hereditary. I have never engaged in any reckless habits that would have this kind of effect on my body. I wondered if this was how my life was going to end. Is it time to lower my coffin six feet into the ground and start shoving the dirt in?

Wait! *No!* This is not me. I do not fear anything. I do not quit! Not me—I am the kid from East Cleveland, Ohio, who excelled in sports and activities in high school. I am the kid who went off to college, then joined the military, served his country, and saw the world. I am the man who married, had children, worked two jobs, and was a part of the best network companies and succeeded.

I am the man who coworkers called "Superman," because after any injury, I bounced back like it was nothing. Yeah, I am the guy who went back to college and made the president and dean's lists every semester. I am the guy who went to work in the oil fields where I had absolutely no experience and moved up quickly in less than six months. Oh, and let's not forget I was the guy who took on a seasonal general labor job then became a certified robotics deployment engineer with no prior experience. I always ended up on top.

All those achievements were part of the personal history I shared with the world. You see, that's what I told myself; that's what everyone knew. *I was the go-to guy.*

So, why am I laying here in a hospital bed questioning myself and having a pity party, when I have accomplished so much in life?

Get up, Jacques!

Get up out of the bed you've been in for a month now, look yourself in the eye, and call yourself a successful, well-established, accomplished man of whom your parents are proud. It's time to have that self-motivation talk and remind yourself *who* you are. Okay, you're here in front of the mirror now. Don't just stand there looking at yourself! You know what to say. Open your mouth and speak your truth. SAY IT, MAN; *go ahead and say it.*

"I AM A CODEPENDENT NARCISSISTIC PATHOLOGICAL LYING FAILURE," I said to the man in the mirror.

WAIT! WHAT?

Yes, I said it, *I am a codependent narcissistic pathological lying failure!* Strong words and a heavy confession, right? Well, it is true, so let me explain.

- Codependent is having an excessive reliance on other people for approval and a sense of identity.

- Narcissistic is when a person has an inflated sense of self-importance.
- A pathological liar tells lies that are defensive and to avoid the consequences of truth-telling
- Failure is simply the lack of success.

So, what does all this mean? How does it pertain to me, you ask? Did I deceive people about my life? Was I just a lonely, needy, lying failure? The answer is "no."

What I saw when I looked in the mirror was this: A man who lied to himself by overinflating his ego because he needed the approval of others when actually he was a complete failure to himself. Everyone on the outside looking in saw the bright shining star, when all that was just on the other side of the glass door was a black hole that was never-ending.

I knew the truth.

Yeah, I was the kid who excelled in sports and activities during high school, but I did so because I felt lonely and trapped, and I'd failed in every other area.

Yeah, I was the kid who went off to college, but I flunked out during my first year.

Yeah, I was the man who joined the military, served his country, and saw the world, and also the guy who went to prison for two-and-a-half years while he was still active duty.

Yeah, I was a married man with three kids, only 21 years old, working two jobs, and I had no idea how to be a husband or father, and my marriage ended in divorce.

Oh, and the network marketing companies? Yeah, about that. Even though I succeeded and shared the stage with some of the greats, I failed miserably at most of them.

Going back to college and excelling was mandatory; I had injured myself so many times that I had to be trained for a new career. But three years and $15,000 later, I never had a chance to enter that new job market.

And I may have moved up quickly when I worked in the oil fields, but every day I endured blatant racism when my coworkers called me "jungle monkey" and hung nooses on trees.

The great robotic deployment job that had me on the road for at least 11 months out of the year? That job separated me from my wife and children so often that my marriage broke up. The separation caused me to lose everything, from my wife and kids to my health and home.

You see, I lied to myself every day, feeding into my own fairy tale, telling myself I was the man with no fears, issues, problems, or concerns, when I had all those things. But my biggest problem was *I bought into my own hype!*

I was Superman, the one who would go out of his way to save the world but could not save himself, because we all know Superman's weakness is kryptonite. In my case, though, I did not realize I was my *own* kryptonite.

My breakthrough came when I finally admitted to myself who the real *me* was. I had never been happy with all the other versions of me because I was never happy with the *real* me. At that breakthrough moment, the most important conversation of my life took place, and it was with myself.

I finally begin to question myself, and I asked a series of questions:

If it bothers me to lie to others, then why is it okay to lie to myself?

Why was I letting myself believe that I was not worthy of my own self-respect and love?

What was it, at that very moment, that finally made me see I had been lying to myself for more than forty years?

Why was I okay with that?

How does this all tie together and what does it mean?

I sat quietly in tears, wondering, *Where did I go wrong and why can't I fix this—and* me?

Then, out of the silence, the voice of the one I call "Daddy" (God) came as clear as day, *"Remember the word you stand on, and make it personal. Instead of saying my name (Lord), say YOU! And add 'I' to refer to yourself. Proverbs 3: 5-6, 'I will trust in YOU with all my heart, and lean not on my own understanding; in all my ways I will acknowledge YOU and YOU will direct my path.'"*

It was at that moment I realized that the thoughts I had of myself were just that, my own thoughts. They were not God's thoughts. *I* called myself those things. *I* was the one who found me unworthy—God never did.

This was about remembering that God placed me here for a reason and with a purpose. And this was about a faith walk in which I had to allow Him to guide my path, because my journey was never about *me*, but about directing the paths of those who will learn from my pitfalls and mistakes.

If I can learn how to be truthful, transparent, open, and honest with myself first, then I can start serving the purpose I was designed for and help those who desperately needed guidance to face the challenges of life.

Now, I did not know how to overcome the fact that I was homeless, having between one and eight seizures every day, and was separated from my family. How was I ever going to get my message out to the world? I needed direction. I wondered how I could serve my purpose if I did not get out of the hospital and find a home.

Funny, as I sit here writing and recalling all of that, I think of how my life and the lives of so many others have changed because I found my truth and know my purpose.

Am I wealthy? It depends on your definition of that word. If you mean financially, then no, but it's coming! If you mean doing what I love and finding ways to help others, then yes!

Am I still homeless? No. Because God has provided shelter each and every day, so I'm not homeless, just houseless.

Am I coping with up to eight seizures a day? No. There's no need to cope with them because I haven't had one in months.

My family, you ask? They surround and support me and my family grows continuously every day.

I no longer worry about my past; I stay laser-focused on my present because that ensures I will achieve a positive and successful future.

I no longer have bad days; I have challenging moments. I live 15 minutes at a time; that way I can never say I've had a bad day if at least 15 minutes of it was good. You see, I changed my principles and my thought processes. I've changed the way I approach life and opened my eyes to my purpose of helping others find theirs.

What you put in the atmosphere is what you get back, and I am living proof! Tony Robbins and others have said, "Change happens when the pain of staying the same is greater than the pain of change."

When I realized change comes easy—with just a decision!— my faith walk became stronger, and serving my purpose became clearer. Everything that happens in my life now makes sense, because now I am able to walk people through the challenges of their lives.

I stopped blaming others for my actions and what I allowed them to do to me, because I realized they only do what I've given them access to do.

Three years ago, I wanted so badly to be mentored by a man I respected and considered a friend, but he told me "no." Not only is he mentoring me now, I work on his team every day, which is the greatest honor for me.

A year ago, I was not sure how I would get my message out to the world, and now I am a co-author with three of the most internationally renowned authors/speakers there are, as well as with other talented people from all over the world. God showed me that my conversation with Johnny Wimbrey three years ago didn't lead to a "no," but instead to a "not right now."

Three years ago, I wasn't ready to learn from a great man of purpose like him. The lies I had told myself had damaged me so much that I was not coachable, teachable, or ready to receive, and it would've been a waste of time and energy for us both. I had to wander through the wilderness for forty years before I could spend my next forty years with you in the Promised Land.

This book is called *Break Through*. I know you're asking yourselves, after all you've read about me, what qualifies me to be a part of this book or gives me the authority to tell you anything on this subject?

The answer is absolutely nothing.

Nothing except this: I have managed to make so many mistakes in my life (and learn from them) that I can at least shorten your learning curve.

Can I help you? Yes! Absolutely! Because when I felt like I was dying because of my own self-inflicted wounds, I learned how to patch myself up and put the oxygen mask on myself first so I could then help and teach all those who feel they are at a loss and about to take their last breath.

Although I'm certified and qualified, I don't refer to myself as a motivational speaker, or a life or transformation coach.

I am simply Jacques Sadler, a "Redirectional Remedy to Life."

Biography

A native of inner city East Cleveland, Ohio, Jacques Sadler spent his summers in the country mountains of Toccoa, Georgia, and quickly learned the value of adapting to his environment in order to survive.

Jacques credits his mother, Gloria Sadler, with teaching him how to be tough, work hard, and fight for everything he wanted; Roy Wilson, the man who adopted him as his son, with giving him the knowledge and skills to be a leader, and to never settle for anything but excellence; and Winston E. Willis, a high-powered African American business man in Cleveland, Ohio, for giving him his first exposure to entrepreneurship and free enterprise.

Jacques excelled in high school, qualifying for state finals two years straight on the Shaw High Speech and Debate Team, in JROTC, selected in the Who's Who Among High School Students Program, and nominated for the Dr. Martin Luther King Jr. Award.

Following high school, Jacques received his first lesson in failure when he flunked out of college in his freshman year, leaving him two options—find employment or enter the military. In 1990, he joined the U.S. Army where he honed his leadership skills and learned discipline.

During his military service, Jacques faced his next big failure—a two-and-a-half-year prison sentence while on active duty. While serving his sentence, Jacques learned about reflection, accepting responsibility, and how to turn a negative situation into a positive one. Jacques believes this period marked the beginning of his developing an overcoming spirit.

Jacques received his introduction to free enterprise and multi-level marketing from Richard and Patricia McGriff and it changed his life and mindset forever. There, Jacques gained his first major success and discovered his gift for sharing his life experiences to help others achieve their goals.

He experienced many ups and downs in business, relationships, and his personal life, but his biggest challenge came three years ago when he developed health problems that caused him to lose his assets, family, and friends.

Through these life-changing moments, Jacques found clarity through loss and learned self-truth. Most importantly, he discovered that we all have an inner power just waiting to be tapped, and he has the ability to help other find their purpose and develop their own plan to attack life.

Contact Information:

Contact Jacques at:
Website: www.JacquesSadler.com
Linkedin/Facebook/Instagram: Jacques Sadler
Email: Jaqargg@gmail.com

CHAPTER ELEVEN

Journey to a Better Life

Deep Laxmi

Be the change you want to see in the world.
—Mahatma Gandhi

My voyage to discover the secrets of living a better life started in 1996, when I picked up a copy of *The Story of My Experiments With Truth: An Autobiography of Gandhi*. This is where I came across the concept of being the change you want to be. The more I said this to myself to understand what it meant, the more it took a shape of its own, and the desire for a better life took hold in my heart.

At that time in my life, I was in a slump. I felt particularly low and hopeless, and my circumstances were not to my liking. It seemed as if there was nothing more to life, as if I didn't matter. A decision needed to be made: Was I going to conform to the societal demands of where I lived, the Dehradun Valley in northern India, or was I going to take off for different circumstances and give my hope a living chance?

When I finally understood the real meaning of "living chance," it ignited my desire to be better, and all the years of studying autobiographies, biographies, and success stories began to connect in my mind. The quest of figuring out why some people are successful always has been of interest to me. It's as if there's a puzzle in my mind just waiting to be solved. My mind was learning how to fly.

I didn't share these new thoughts with anyone because I was afraid to be judged, criticized, or simply called crazy.

My own self-talk did not help me. On one side, I'd hear an inner voice say, "Girls can't do this, girls are not supposed to do that," and on the other side I would hear, "There is a better place, there is a better life, you can do better."

Because I read so much, all the inspirational stories and the inner voice saying, *There is a better place and you can do better*, took hold in my mind, and the negative voices saying what girls *couldn't* do finally faded away, but not without some resistance.

I was also the victim of an inferiority complex and believed everybody else knew and were more successful, and I was just not smart enough to understand things. Feeling that way left me afraid of speaking out and appearing even dumber. Because I had also been called a crybaby and unlucky many times, I didn't want to appear any sadder or dumber than I already believed I was.

I had a *very* negative self-image. I didn't value myself enough, but the desire to find a better life was very much there and was starting to develop strong roots. I wanted to give my faith a chance.

Lesson: Self-image is the most important thing, we never outperform our own self-image. (How is your self-image? How do you see yourself? How do you talk to yourself? What's your choice of words when you talk to yourself)?

Having the desire to have a better life had taken root. I nurtured it by studying. I became a listening and reading machine and closed my mind to everything else. When I faced certain unpleasant situations or someone would say something contradictory to my beliefs, instead of confronting them, I poured my thoughts into my journal.

I did not listen to negative comments from others. I was determined to find peace and let my mind take many flights in the autobiographies and writings of those who have achieved great success in life.

Lesson: Close the doors of your mind to all that is not serving you.

Once I fully understood the change I desired to make, I started my search for what change meant for me and began to work on my journey toward building a better life. Studying the law of success and anyone who has achieved success became my life's passion.

I discovered the first step I needed to make for these changes was to set a goal.

My father once said, "If you shoot for the moon, you will end up in the stars." Now this was at a time when the word "shoot" created a picture of a bow and arrow, not a gun. I think in pictures, so I built a picture of his words: A little girl in a white frock shooting for the moon with a bow and arrow. Somehow the arrow touched the moon and ended up on the bed of stars. This visual has been a great source of inspiration to me.

I decided upon my breakthrough goal: My first goal—*my moon*—was to get out of my parents' house without having to marry someone. You may think, what kind of goal this is? What's the big deal?

If you were a girl in northern India at that time, even a well-educated city girl, you were expected to settle down and be married to a suitable boy by the time you were 20 or 22 years old (if not earlier). That's what your relatives and society expected of you and of your parents.

By the way, I despised the term *settle down* then, and I still do. It sounds as if you are going to be made into a tree and planted into ground for the rest of your life. I am not a tree, so settling down is not for me, but I didn't share these thoughts, with anyone but only with my journal and the other term I don't particularly like is *falling in love*. Why would someone *fall* in love? Love is a great emotion; one should *fly* in love. Somehow, the word *fly* always has been a source of inspiration to help me reach new heights in my imagination.

Lesson: If you don't like something in your life, change it.

As I grew older, I learned you become what you think about all day long. In moments of reflection, I find myself extremely blessed and grateful to my mother. One of her ongoing suggestions has always been to keep your mind calm, think good thoughts. Despite my usual adverse situation, I was able to regain my mental strength and remind myself to follow my mother's advice. My inclination to read books and watch inspirational movies was a constant source of support for a better future. A favorite movie is *Gandhi*; another is *Chariots of Fire*, which contains one of my favorite quotes:

Where does the power come from? Power comes from within.

Lesson: Self-talk is of utmost important, we become what we think about.

As a man thinketh in his heart so is he.

My tests in life were only beginning, there were only two acceptable ways for me to get out of my parents' house alive, either by getting married to a person of my parents' choice (which I didn't want) or being accepted by some university for further education. Yes, there was a third choice—run away—but this choice was not very appealing to me for various reasons.

My supportive big brothers broke the barrier by moving away from home; while that was a help, it also came with constant reminders: "They are boys and you are a girl."

My decision to move away was a firm one, yet it still was a secret. I had total faith that somehow this was going to happen. I was going to achieve my goal, though I didn't know how. I was operating from the place of *knowing* which came with faith and total belief. There was no shadow of doubt in my mind or in my heart, though I didn't have words to explain this total belief.

At times dark thoughts try to invade my mind, but my desire for the grass to be greener and the sky to be bluer was so strong, that nothing else could take root in my mind. During this time, my mother, the Bible, and Bhagavad Gita, a sacred Hindu text, were of great help.

Three not-quite-real words helped make my belief stronger with each passing day: Picturize, Prayerize, and Actualize.

> I slept and dreamt that life was joy.
> I awoke and saw that life was service.
> I acted and behold, service was joy.
> **—Rabindranath Tagore**

Later in life, I discovered that persistence is one of the non-negotiable traits in every single successful person. Napoleon

Hill wrote, "Persistence is to the character of man as carbon is to steel." You can put this to acid test, whether it's successful people around you or even the success you have achieved in life. You'll find this success came as a result of constant action on a daily basis toward a definite purpose.

My persistence, along with lots of help from my beloved brothers, and unconditional love and support from my rock—my mother—was constant. I knew my father had my best interest at heart, because he gave me the best education and walked an extra mile to do so, and that had to fulfill some greater purpose. Finally the day came where he decided to let me fly solo.

Yes! My breakthrough moment. I could not have done it if my dad was not okay with it.

As I said, my tests in life were just beginning after learning that my dream was finally a reality. I was still speechless and unable to express that feeling, that it truly was happening. I decided to celebrate with my friends, all of the people I was about to leave behind.

The celebration was on January 1, 2000, a memorable day. On my way back home after the celebration, I had a scooter accident. I still very vividly remember hitting my head three times on the road. This near-death experience was a turning point in life.

I was lying in the middle of the road on my back; everything appeared cloudy and all the noises were muffled, just like they show in movies. Well, in my real-life movie, I could see people looking at me and talking but no one was helping me to get up.

Then I heard this faint voice which grew louder and clearer every second, "*Didi ko uthao, didi ko uthao* (pick up my big sister, pick up my big sister)." Then I felt people were finally lifting me up and moving me.

My accident was right in front of the medical clinic. God works in mysterious ways, you know. People took me to the clinic where the doctor bandaged me up and I drove back home.

Later that night, my mother found me unconscious with blood all over the pillow. She reached out to my uncle for help, and he took me to the emergency room. There, the doctor had to shave part of my head to reach the wound, nine stitches in total. As he was stitching, my uncle was praising me to the doctor, saying, "She is a good girl, and she is going to America for her Ph.D."

As the doctor heard this, he stopped stitching and said, "She is not going anywhere, she has lost a lot of blood. She will die if she travels."

I wasn't quiet. I told the doctor, "I trust you to do your job, but you must tell me how I can take care of myself. I *have* to go; I *must* go. The decision was made. I am willing to do whatever I have to do for me to live my goal. See, it is now or never for me."

The doctor said, "Daughter, with your will, you can do anything. My father has often used this idiom, 'where there is a will there is a way.' When you are willing to do your best, miracles are achieved. This was the test of will.

Lesson: Give your goal all you got, with all your might.

I must tell you about the boy who saved my life by asking people to pick me up. My mother taught me a saying, "Do the good deeds and don't think about them." Very early on during my school and college days, I used to stop by an orphanage on a regular basis to give the little kids some candies, and later on pencils and notebooks. The smiles on the children's faces were very fulfilling and rewarding. Life seemed worthwhile, and it felt as if I mattered, and my life had a purpose.

The boy who saved me was from that very orphanage and he reminded me that I had also helped him get the job as a mechanic in the shop next to the clinic. God could not have chosen a better place for that accident; he also appointed the angels to save me.

Be true to yourself and to your goal, and everything standing in your way will give up one way or the other. Forge ahead in the direction of your dreams, do not stop until you reach them.

You can have everything in life you want,
if you will just help other people get what they want.
—Zig Ziglar

Lesson: Once you have decided on a goal, commit until you reach it.

Action Steps: Take at least three action steps toward your goal every day. Being successful is a process, and though it is hard, it is all worth it; you are worth it.

Biography

Deep Laxmi has excelled in business for the past 15 years as a pharmaceutical quality professional. She holds three postgraduate degrees, an MBA from St. Joseph University, an M.S. from Georgia State University, an M.S. from Agra University, and dozens of professional certifi cates.

She is passionate about helping others to fulfill their dreams and to live an abundant and intentional life. After studying personal growth and development for more than twenty-five years, Deep has turned her passion into a business, Self-Image Academy, and is a mentor, author, and speaker who helps people boost productivity. As a certified leadership coach, she has trained and coached clients, including teens, to achieve better self-image, attitude, career selections, performance, and growth. She teaches them to set big, worthy goals, change their self-image, and turn old habits into new lifelong successful habits for an abundant and purpose-driven life. The fast-growing Self-Image Academy currently serves clients in three continents.

After being rescued by an orphan in 2000, Deep gives back to orphans throughout the world by providing education, shelter, and entrepreneurial skills, and she financially supports many children in India and the United States. As a wife, mother of three young boys, pharmaceutical professional, and director of the Academy, balancing work/life/passion is the challenge she wakes up to and looks forward to everyday.

Contact Information:

Website: selfi mageacademy.com
Email: info@selfi mageacademy.com

CHAPTER TWELVE

In My Parents' Footsteps

Patrick Brown

On the day my soul was broken, I was also encouraged by the renewal of my spirit. A few days before my mother's death, my siblings and I went to Mexia, Texas, to visit my mother in the hospital. Our dad told us that he and our mother had agreed she was ready to go be with the Lord.

That was the last time we as a family prayed together with Mother. When we were younger, Daddy would gather us together and each one of us would pray an individual prayer. At my mother's sickbed, though, I prayed and cried along with my siblings. I remember praying with my eyes open so I could see my mother's face while she lay in bed. She had a warm, loving, and gracious smile and the clear understanding that she was going to a better place. That knowledge gave me a peace that is still with me this day.

A few days later I went to work, and on the way, I prayed and cried and prayed and cried, not knowing that God already had answered my prayer. Later while I was working, I received a phone call, and when I heard the phone ring, I knew my mother had passed. My daughter and son-in-law came to pick me up and asked me gently if I was okay.

Strangely enough, I did feel fine, and I reassured them I was well.

We drove straight to the hospital. When we entered my mother's room, I saw she still had the same smile and there was peace on her face. I closed my eyes and bowed my head, and I too felt peace, knowing that she was in a better place.

It was important to my father that all of us were a part of my mother's burial process. We went with him to the funeral home, and after we talked with the funeral director, we went with him to look at caskets. I immediately noticed a beautiful, elegant brown casket, and as we walked by it, I stopped and knew it was the one my father would pick, so I didn't bother to inspect any other caskets. Though I can't say why, this one reminded me of a Mother's Day when I was much younger.

On that long-ago Mother's Day, Mom picked out an outfit to wear and laid it on the bed beside Daddy's suit. Daddy came and saw what Mother was planning to wear, and he picked up the outfit and looked at it closely. He told her it was not good enough for his wife and left. Later he came back with a brand-new outfit, a much nicer one, that he'd bought her to wear on that special day.

I was too young to understand clothing that long-ago Mother's Day, but I was the right age to understand love. When I saw the luxurious-looking brown casket, I knew it was the one, and that casket was the one Daddy picked. He loved her in death as much as he loved her in life.

It was cold on the day of my mother's burial, and there was ice on the ground, so several people did not attend due to the weather. I was somewhat confused in my spirit; I felt no sorrow, no pain, and no loss in my heart. People were telling me that the day of the funeral is when the grieving really starts.

During the funeral and as we laid her to rest, my heart remained the same, untouched by pain. When my family finally got in the car to go home, tears began to run down my face. At that moment, remembering my mother's smile and how much joy it brought me along with her courage and grace, I felt a great sense of peace.

I have some additional peace with another memory of that day, thinking about the cold weather and understanding that cold preserves. To me, the cold weather was God's way of giving me confirmation that my mother will be preserved for the day of redemption and telling me that she still is.

Since my mother's death, I have often wondered how my parents' lives have affected me and I must say GOD is good. Through my mother's death, I now understand I really want to go to Heaven. My father is still alive and he is still showing me how to live on this earth and prepare myself for the rest of my journey to get there.

Some years later when my father remarried, his marriage caused quite a bit of dissent in the family. There were multiple reasons, since each sibling had to work out how to accept the change within their own spirit. I was in my late 40s—the youngest in the family—and it was the first time I felt my family's peace was broken. The discord was not because of the woman my father married, because she was a good woman and we didn't resent her. It was a result of radically changing the family structure after more than 45 years being a single unit.

There was no question having a stepmother takes some getting used to, no matter who or how good she might be, or how much she loved my father. I knew and accepted my mother and father as my parents—as one entity in two different bodies, because I had never seen or heard them conduct themselves in any other way.

They even dealt with my mother's final illness as a single unit, and I had never been asked by either of them to help care for my mother while she went through her cancer treatments and all the difficult consequences. They only reached out when they knew it was a serious situation, which again showed me they were one in the flesh, which the scriptures say they should be.

After carefully observing and listening to family members struggling with the death of my mother, I approached one of my brothers and suggested we create a new tradition of having family reunions. We hoped a reunion would help heal at least a portion of the pain experienced by family members. We believed the most important thing to do was to create a family order, because God told us how it should be done.

Let all things be done decently and in order.

—**I Corinthians 14:40** (King James Version)

We all needed to understand that we could not bring Mother back, but we could set an order ordained by God that will lead us into his rest.

Leading up to our first family reunion, we were meeting once a month to discuss and plan the event, but we found we also discussed matters we had never talked about before. Sometimes, our discussions caused us to ask why we hadn't done this when Mother was still living, but then the Holy Ghost revealed to me that we didn't need it when she was here;

you only need to fill a hole when it is empty.

The first two years after Daddy's remarriage were very stressful for us siblings, but God knew that for us to get past the issue, we first needed to be willing to accept change on Daddy's terms, not ours. We finally realized that for us to really heal, we must be willing to discuss and work out some things that we never had to deal with.

I am truly at peace with my mother's death and the decision that my dad made to remarry. It is not my place to add any discomfort to my dad's life and I chose not to. The family reunion has been a great spiritual and psychological eye-opener for our family, all four generations, and we've had a series of breakthroughs.

We learned a great deal about how we deal with conflict, with loss, and with change. We accepted and must continue to understand that *we* don't choose our family—*God* does that. Finally, the family completely grasped the meaning of the verse: **What** therefore **God** hath **joined together**, let not man put asunder (Mark 10:9, KJV).

We continue to have reunions once every year.

❯❯ ❮❮

All my life, I have done my best to follow in my parents' footsteps.

As far back as I can remember, my parents had extended family living with us. I say "extended" family because my oldest step-sister was so close to me that I did not know she was not my biological sister until my teenage years. Her son and another young man also stayed in the house. My parents treated everyone as family. Daddy always knew of someone who was in need, and he did not hesitate to connect us with them, young or old. Looking back over our lives, our mom and dad taught us the meaning of "church" right in our home environment. The devil cannot break a family that he has no power over.

I started playing organized sports when I was nine years old and began coaching my nephews and other youths when I was 15. Playing sports combined with the structured life my parents maintained for us became a protective hedge God had grown around me.

My family lived in an area of Ft. Worth known as "Stop Six" or "Eastwood." My future wife was at that time living on the Southside. Though both neighborhoods were dangerous communities with dangerous people, no one messed with our sports teams. Despite what was happening in both communities, at no time did anyone I encountered ever try to force any of the athletes to join gangs, do drugs, or engage in anything else that would have harmed us. Even when I was just 12 it was obvious to me that sports have a power for good within a community.

We go through life not understanding why and what we are here for, but the earlier we figure it out, the more time we can have a positive impact on society.

That early understanding of the importance of sports within a community has led me to a lifetime commitment to youth sports.

It gives me great pleasure to talk now about my own wife and children. In Proverbs 18:22 (KJV), God said, *Who so findeth a wife, findeth a good thing*. My wife, Felicia, embodies good every day of her life in every action and word, and I appreciate her love and goodness every day of my life.

Scripture also tells us: *Train up a child in the way he should go:*

and when he is old, he will not depart from it (Proverbs 22:6, KJV). My children have not departed. As adults, they are as great a part of my life as my siblings and I were of my parents' lives. My children and their children bring my wife and me peace, love, and happiness every day of our lives.

While I was dealing with my mother's illness and dying, my wife and children added no extra pressure or stress on me. They all supported me during this painful time in many small but meaningful ways.

Anybody who knows my wife knows she must be dressed perfectly to leave the house, and this can take some time. The day Mother died, I left work to go home and pick up my wife, son, and granddaughters to view my mothers' body before it was moved from the hospital room. When I told my wife it was time to go, she calmly said, "Yes, sir," without any questions and without gathering the million items she would normally take with her and got into the car.

To my wife and children, I give my appreciation and gratitude for not disturbing my heart while I was going through that difficult time in my life.

Biography

Patrick Brown is a multi-directional influential leader who has inspired over 30,000 residents of Fort Worth, Texas, and his purpose is to bridge the gaps among the community, church, school, and police department. His mission is to revitalize the village model for his community that integrates diversity and promotes trusted relationships and unity. He believes "a synergized community builds prosperity!" Patrick gives back freely of what he's been given, and he remains committed to bringing the best out of people within his community.

Widely known as a coach, entrepreneur, leader, and youth advocate, some of Patrick's community responsibilities include serving as President of the Oscar Dean Wyatt High School PTA, a board member for the United Neighborhood Association, President of the Southside Hornets, and the Commissioner and Program Director of the Fort Worth Police Athletic League (PAL). Devoted to elevating his community, Patrick developed programs tailored to the members' habitual needs such as: Understanding-the Needs-In-Today's-Youth (UNITY), Graceful-Leaders-Understanding-Education (GLUE), Triple Threat Sports Club, and Parents-And-Students-Success (PASS). Patrick currently is teaming up with the FW Sparc to create the first ever after-school Youth Sports Standards.

As a grassroots business owner for more than 38 years, Patrick works tirelessly, searching for and creating opportunities that will catapult small community youth businesses toward success. As the author of the Fort Worth UNITY Program, he instituted progressive developmental platform to empower youth to look beyond their obstacles and to reach their full potential.

Additionally, his diverse expertise and devoted passion to the community has solidified his partnerships with corporations such as the ACH Child and Family Services in Fort Worth, Fort Worth Police Department, Fort Worth PAL, Fort Worth Independent School District, the Rainwater Foundation, and many more community programs. Patrick believes that great opportunities and partnerships are made as a result of great relationships and says, "We must change the game on how we see others within our community relationships."

Among Patrick's achievements are development of a five-year plan for the Fort Worth Police Department in 2016, being named the Father of the Year Hall of Fame inductee in 2017 by the Fatherhood Coalition, receiving a Community Youth Supporter Certificate in 2017 from the Fort Worth Independent School District, receiving the 2018 Community Engagement Award from the Fort Worth Police Athletic League, and being named a 2019 Youth Sports Honoree by the FWISD Athletics Department.

Patrick continuously advises and empowers the community, church, school, and police department. He motivates his coaches and mentees to execute their vision; building resilient mentors that are mentally, physically, and spiritually prepared to stimulate community cohesion. Patrick cultivates an environment where everyone within the community has a purpose and together, they will build prosperity.

Patrick and his wife, Felicia (Dial) Brown, live in Ft. Worth, Texas, near their son, Patrick (Dial) Brown. The couple's daughter, Latisha Ireland, has served in the U.S. Air Force for more than 16 years. Latisha and her husband have three daughters, Kaleia, Jaila, and Ivy.

Contact information

Email: Coachpatrick83@aol.com
Facebook: patrick.brown.98837

CHAPTER THIRTEEN

Embrace Your Inner Superhero

Roni M. Benjamin

As a single mother in the Astoria Housing Projects in New York City, my mom worked late hours to provide for her children, and she held down two jobs to make ends meet. After school, my evenings were spent in home daycare in my neighborhood. In first grade, I had little homework, so I would complete my assignments, eat dinner, and rest until my mother finished her second job and could pick me up.

The caregiver was an older woman, and I do not remember any other children in her home. What I remember is two nights. A man—a monster, really—took me off the couch and made me go into the bathroom. The man forced me to lean over in the bathtub while he raped me. The pain was horrible. Sixyear-old bodies are not meant to do adult things. I could not understand why he did what he did, but understood it was a terrible, secret thing.

The Monster covered my mouth so no one could hear my cries. My tears rolled down my face like a waterfall.

I could not believe that no one cared what the Monster was doing with a child in the bathroom late at night. How could it be that no one came looking for me? The Monster wiped me clean, dried my tears, and cleaned my face so no one would see my pain and distress.

The second night was worse—what he did to my body was so terrible he could not clean me up enough to hide all the evidence. Mom picked me up as usual. We went home, she undressed me to get me prepared for a bath, and noticed the blood in my panties. She was crying, with tears rolling down her face, and gently pleaded with me to tell her what happened. Finally, I told her what the Monster had done to me for two nights. I told her how he pulled me into the bathroom, pulled my clothes off, bent me over the bathtub, and hurt me.

My mother was my saving grace. She literally saved my life I felt like she woke me up from a nightmare. Why didn't I tell her sooner? I never went back to that horrible house of horror.

The police made a report and took my clothing as evidence. Time went by and I remember having to appear before a judge and attorneys to describe the events that occurred over those two nights and answer questions, so many questions. My mother gave me the confidence and strength to tell the same story I told her the night of the second attack. Holding a dark-colored doll made of cloth, I demonstrated the things the Monster did to me. I can still feel the pain and relief of sharing my truth; it is very similar to how I am feeling as I write this. In my child's mind and heart, I knew justice would prevail, that the Monster would get his day of reckoning. I was sure of it.

But that is not what happened.

The Monster never served time for what he did. Why not? His girlfriend testified before God that he was with her on both nights and gave him an alibi. I thought the Monster would pay for his actions and be punished for the pain he caused me.

Instead, he remained a free man.

I immediately felt pain and fear for other girls he may have hurt because of his freedom. It is a throat-clogging hard pill to swallow. You know what helped me heal and forgive them both? I read, "Do not avenge yourselves, beloved, but yield place to the wrath; for it is written: 'Vengeance is mine; I will repay,' says Jehovah." (Romans 12:19, New World Translation of the Holy Scriptures, 2013 Revision.)

And so, I left it to God.

My brother Corey is three years older than I am, and he had his own battles within himself as he grew up. He was in and out of group homes for most of his life. I can only imagine the challenges he faced in these strange places with other boys dealing with their own internal struggles. It is possible that what he experienced in those places may have pushed 11-year-old Corey to sexually assault me, his 8-year-old sister. He may have been acting out what someone else taught him to do. However, there is no excuse. It is sick and I will never understand it. Thankfully, he did not stay home long enough for those terrible nights to last long.

When he was about 14 or 15, he came home again and was in his right state of mind. At that time, my mom was dating Jan, the amazing man who helped mom raise us. Jan's presence in the home was a positive influence on Corey. Jan challenged him to dream big, set goals, and aspire to greatness. Corey slowly became a better person and made some good friends. He protected me from the knuckleheads in the neighborhood and I started to see his love for me. He never touched me in an inappropriate way ever again. God was listening to my prayers.

Corey became my biggest supporter with all my activities. He took me to my track events and cheered me on as I raced to the finish lines. He invited his friends to the house to hear me sing. He thought I had a gift. I knew without a shadow of a doubt my brother loved me and felt remorse for his behavior when we were younger. He became my very best friend.

As he grew older, though, his troubles seemed to get worse. He got himself into some serious trouble in his teenage years and it cost him his freedom. I never knew what crime he committed to warrant jail time. However, I believe being locked up gave him time to think and work on a plan to get his life together. When he was 19 years old, he got his freedom papers, came back home, got a job, and was on a good path. We were proud of the direction his life was taking.

Then came October 11, 1995. I was 16. I had track and dance practice as I did every day after school. Mel, my high school boyfriend, always traveled with me back home. Every day he took at least two trains and a bus to get from his home in Harlem to where I lived in Queens.

When I arrived home at about 9 p.m., our apartment was full of people I did not recognize. At first, I thought it might be a party of some sort. When I looked closely into the eyes of these strangers, however, I saw something was wrong. In a blink of an eye my mother was walking toward me with her arms extended and I saw sorrow and pain in her eyes. She held me tight and I instantly knew it was Corey.

"What happened?" I asked. "Is he going to be okay?"

"He's gone, Roni! Corey is gone," my mother sobbed.

I fell to the floor and cried for what felt like an eternity. My life as I knew it was over. I lost my brother, my friend, and my protector. I remember running downstairs to where I last saw his friends. Surely, they would be able to tell me more about what happened, right? But they either could not or would not tell me what happened. I do not remember much of that night after that point. I was a mess for a long time.

The reality of my brother's death came at the funeral services five days later. I was at his casket talking to him and praying for my own strength when someone pulled me away from him, and this triggered the pain deep down and allowed it to resurface. My last goodbye had been cut short too soon.

For the next year, my life was very dark and lonely. I distanced myself from my friends and people who loved me without realizing I was doing it. My mother and Jan could not function through the pain of losing Corey. Their relationship was never the same. The world around me crumbled.

My mother knew she needed to do something drastic to help me, so she sent me to stay with cousins in North Carolina. There I finally found deliverance from my depression and darkness. My cousin Tammy prayed for me, her children, my cousins Devin, Daryln, and their siblings comforted me through my ordeal. I remember we were having praise and worship and the song *Going Up Yonder (to be with my Lord)* came on, and I sang until the tears rolled down my face. I could feel the weight of the world lift off me and the sun started to shine again in my life.

I believe that moment was a major breakthrough for me. I let go and let my brother's soul rest with the Lord. I finally had the strength to pick myself up, dust myself off, and continue with the life I was given. I went back home to New York City, and graduated from high school.

⤜•⤛

Traces of the pain of living with sexual abuse and without a father being present resurfaced in many areas of my life. My relationships with men were strongly affected. I attracted men who were hurt and broken, and tried to change them. When I look back at that time, I realize I believed my love could fix anyone.

My two marriages were marred by physical abuse. The first abuser danced with me in the moonlight on our first date. I felt like the luckiest woman alive. Year one was filled with happy memories. It was not until my son, who was four years old at the time, and I moved in with "Moonlight" that I began to see a different side of him. One minute, he was kind and gentle, the next angry and confrontational. I remember fights because of his deep-routed insecurity and jealousy. There was constant yelling, pushing, and shoving. It was the first time I had experienced domestic violence in my own home.

I knew then the future boded trouble for us, yet I did not leave. Arguments and fights continued, layered with good times and peaceful moments. The longer we stayed together, the more aggressive the fights became. Police were called. I would leave for a night and return. Then, he began pulling the phone out of the wall when I tried to call the police.

When he punched me in my eye, I knew I had to get out of there. The following day, I washed clothes and packed up my car when he was at work. I moved to Delaware, found refuge n my mother's home with my (now) two kids, and divorced Moonlight.

Then I met "Comforter," who turned out to be sick with the disease of alcoholism. Only sixty days after we were married, we had our first argument over how he disciplined my son, who was twelve at the time. Comforter was upset by our argument, which was his excuse to drink until he was intoxicated while I was at work and the children were at school. After I came home from work and put the kids to bed, Comforter physically abused me. He bit me, punched me, and threw me across the room with all his considerable strength.

I thought I would die when he choked me to the point that I almost passed out, and I screamed "Jehovah"—that is all I had the strength to do. When he heard the name, Comforter released his grasp, fell to the bed, curled into a fetal position, and cried himself to sleep. I grabbed my children and left. He called me the next morning and asked, "What happened last night? The room is a disaster. Did I hurt you?" I knew then I had gone from the furnace straight into the fire.

Life for us was never the same after that. He promised to stop drinking and agreed no alcohol would ever enter the house. He went to drug and alcohol counseling for about a month.

One day, I came home, saw a case of beer in the refrigerator, and asked about our agreement not to have alcohol in the home.

"It's just beer, for goodness sake," he said, dismissing my question.

After eight months, I made the decision to get out of the marriage because I could not risk another near-death experience.

After my divorce, I moved back to Georgia to work on a better relationship with Moonlight. After all, I reasoned, we had raised two kids together; after four years of being apart, surely there was growth and maturity, right? Our relationship was better for two years. We decided to remarry. One year later, the arguments resumed and I felt unsupported, unappreciated, and devalued.

The end came after he slammed the door in my mother's face and told her she was not welcome in his house. My mother had moved from Delaware to Texas to show her absolute support for our remarriage. She had supported us physically, mentally, monetarily, and emotionally since the remarriage, yet Moonlight was disrespectful to her non-stop.

In 2016, I packed my things and left, never to return. Moonlight and I now parent our two children from two separate households of peace rather than from one of chaos.

⧓ ⧓

My next breakthrough came when I was asked by my life coach and friend to write a letter to my younger self, a letter telling her whatever I thought she should know.

"Write it, read it, then destroy the letter," my friend said.

The letter was my attempt to let go of the past and move on with my future. And to my surprise, the letter became my first step in healing my soul.

Then I was introduced to the world of network marketing, which helped me begin a lifetime of personal development. Les Brown's audio recordings reminded me there was greatness within me. Johnny Wimbrey told me in his audios that the only one who can stop me from pursuing my goals and dreams was me. If I wanted to see changes in my life, I knew I would have to do things differently. I read a lot of empowering books to reinforce my belief that I can create the life I have always wanted for myself.

In addition to running my own business, I began acting and am now a cast member of the award-winning stage play Soul Purpose. My journey to become an effective public speaker began and went well, and now I am the president of

Intuit Toastmasters, where I coach other Toastmasters on their development as communicators. I am the new co-host on RedBoi Raydio, which is soon to be syndicated, playing old school hip hop and R&B, and sharing triumphant messages around the world. I sit on the board of Soul Reborn, a 501(c)(3) organization that addresses the personal and professional development needs of women who are unable to achieve professional success due to personal hurt, unforgiveness, grief, loss, or low self-esteem.

I am raising my children to be future leaders, go-getters, fearless, and goal-driven entrepreneurs. I intend to share my story of victim to victory at every turn. My goal is to empower, inspire, and motivate others to embrace the inner superhero that lies dormant, waiting on us to activate our powers.

Biography

Roni M. Benjamin was born in Queens, New York City, where she and her older brother were raised in the housing projects by her single mother. At a young age, Roni was exposed to drugs, rape, molestation, and murder, and her experiences led to a lifestyle of promiscuity, self-doubt, and emptiness. Her writing gives insight to how she endured through the trials of being a mother at a young age, a broken heart, domestic violence, and her search for true love.

She has two remarkable children, Corey, 19, and Summer, 11.

Roni is an entrepreneur, author, radio personality and life coach. Her passion is fueled by her deep desire to inspire others to reach their fullest potential in life.

Contact Information:

Web: www.ronimbenjamin.com
Email: Ronimbenjamin@live.com

CHAPTER FOURTEEN

C'Est l'Histoire d'un Gars
(This Is the Story of a Guy)

Steven Bourgeois

Being curious in nature, I asked myself some existential questions at an early stage of my life. It was the "Who are we? What are we doing here on earth? What is the purpose of life?" kind of stuff.

This led me to dreams and more questions I asked myself: "Where do dreams come from? Why are some people not dreaming while others only remember parts of it? Where does the conscious go when we fall asleep and become unconscious?"

When I was 18 years old and studying how the brain works and the invisible (parapsychology), I attended a Tony Robbins event that introduced me to neuro-linguistic programming (NLP). The event was a revelation and game-changer for my life. Tony is still part of my daily routine 30 years later.

NLP is an approach to communication, personal development, and psychotherapy. According to Wikipedia, NLP's creators claim there is a connection between neurological processes (neuro-), language (linguistic), and behavioral patterns learned through experience (programming), and they can be changed to achieve specific goals in life.

Let me say I am not a gazillionaire—just the guy next door.

Some consider me successful because I do what I want most of the time, but my definition of success is not measured in a dollar amount, but rather in terms of happiness. To me, success is doing all you want, being free to decide with whom, when, and where you want to be. Others call this financial freedom.

So, for this chapter, I will not be talking about the dreams we experience during sleep, but rather the dreams such as when we contemplate the possibility of doing something unknown.

I remember being sixteen years old, making a list of things I wanted to have, be, and do. I remember being nineteen, realizing all I wanted on that list from two years earlier—all those dreams—were part of my daily life. I understood even then that mindset is the foundation of everything, and I started using affirmations to reprogram my habits and beliefs.

Affirmations? It's when I repeat a sentence—up to 100 times per day—so many times that it becomes a new belief inside of me. Eventually, that affirmation becomes my reality because I learned you must see and feel it inside your mind first before seeing it outside in your life.

I am passionate about setting goals, achieving goals, and state of mind. I believe that daily and consistent personal development is crucial for growth. Finding coaches and mentors is a must for success because what we experience in life is always the result of our thinking.

If I were to make a list of inspirational audios, I'd include

Bob Proctor conclusions, Dale Carnegie influences, Napoleon Hill thinking, Ekhart Tolle feelings, Robert Anthony teachings, Wallace D. Wattles sciences, Wayne Dyer words of wisdom, and Gary Vee repetitions.

I am a big believer that it requires the same energy to make $10,000 or $100,000, per year, per month, or per week—it does not matter. What is important is to clearly define your goals and then it is all about action.

Massive action = massive results.

(The universe will give you what you feel.)

To win in life, we must work on our self-talk and mindset more than our craft. Nobody can put limits on us or our success. We can do anything we want just by believing in ourselves. All we need for change, growth, and transformation is already in us.

- How about your goals and dreams?
- How is your plan working out so far?
- Are you where you should be?

Obstacles are the path to success

In 1999, I had been traveling in France for 30 days when I chose to stay in Europe for five-plus years. This happened again in 2006 when I was traveling in Vietnam for 60 days and I stayed in Asia for five-plus years. People call this the "laptop lifestyle" now. I have been living this life for more than twenty years.

The early days of the internet made me a successful entrepreneur in 1996. I needed a vacation after the organization of the first webmasters meeting in Montreal back in 1999. I landed in Paris on July 13 and stayed near the Versailles castle for the July 14 fireworks (their national day). I had been in that area for a week before someone recommended I visit the Alps because I like mountains. That is how I experienced my first high-speed train.

I was looking for an internet connection to check my emails, and I came across a guy who welcomed me with open arms. He introduced me to his mountains where I had a feeling of déjà-vu, and I decided to settle there. I paid for a plane ticket for a friend who brought my dog from America to Europe, and I started a new life.

I spent a few years in Grenoble, the capital of the French Alps, and I learned to paraglide. Amsterdam was my second home and I traveled all around Europe until I sold my company in 2004, using this opportunity to start all over again for the second time.

On my birthday in late 2006, I landed in Da Nang, Vietnam, and remained there a few years. Those were the best years of my life in one sense; on the other hand, I stopped focusing daily on personal growth, and I lost track of myself. At some point, I left my comfortable beachfront lifestyle to relocate in Sapa for an adventure that changed my life.

In "the city in the clouds" near the Chinese border, I felt great empathy for the ethnic minority children begging in the streets and I imagined solutions to improve the life of those local communities. (My work on taphin.com is still online.)

With a work contact and work permit in hand, I was ready to proceed when the authorities asked me to leave the country and return with a business visa. So, I went to Bangkok for a weekend and had a surprise at the immigration office which had a "no visa for you" policy when I tried to return.

Without any explanations from the embassy, I was stuck in Thailand with no clothes and no way in returning home to Vietnam. I was forced to start over again, but for the first time, starting over was against my will. It made me evaluate my whole life, as my universe seemed to be falling apart.

While creating original campaigns to contribute to the education of ethnic minority children and providing long-term solutions focused on responsible tourism, I concluded that a partnership with an existing foundation would be a more judicious solution than creating my own foundation.

Back in my home country of Canada, I isolated myself in a cabin, focused on reprogramming myself, and building new streams of income until one day, I had a life-changing event.

My personal breakthrough?

While I continued working on my indigenous project 12,000 miles away, I joked to my dad, "I am now as poor as the ethnic minorities I am trying to get out of poverty"—and it hit me like a brick. I *had* become like the people I was trying to help. I had become them.

Have you ever heard the expression, "You are the average of the five people you spend the most time with?"

I had been living in the rice paddies with the Hmong and Dao tribes, where everything around me was poverty and injustice. I was talking to charitable organizations about fundraising. I was focused on finding solutions to poverty. I was talking poverty and I was feeling poverty—and so I became poor.

The thing is, it is not easy to think about health when you are surrounded by disease or to think about riches when you are in the presence of misery. Doing so requires a power I forgot was inside me.

Realizing that, I changed my focus and everything changed. Suddenly, I understood that to erase poverty, we must not embed pictures of poverty into our mind, but instead embed pictures of wealth and abundance into the minds of the poor.

That is how and when I decided to become rich because I finally realized it is the best way I can help the poor. All that was needed was to reprogram my financial footprint and believe in the goal already achieved.

My business breakthrough?

At this exact same time, after 20 years of working in affiliate marketing, I discovered the multi-level marketing industry. Let's define the difference between the two:

Affiliate Marketing—Where people make commissions when they introduce a product/service to customers. Only one level, just me; I get paid only for my sales and nobody else's sales.

Network Marketing—MLM, or Multi-Level Marketing. Same as above plus I can build a team that pays me on multiple levels because I earn a percentage of the team's sales. The result is volume = leverage.

I had an affiliate mindset when I joined a gold company late 2013 and did not understand the value of network marketing. It was the same way when I first discovered Bitcoin; I did not understand the technology behind the blockchain at the beginning.

To make a long story short, it was about a year later that I logged in again and saw points in my first gold account.

Tons of units accumulated and are still accumulating, and it came from people in my team, not me doing anything. One of my team members was a real leader because he introduced us to hundreds, and I had all these people under me creating points in my account.

That is how I really discovered the multi-level marketing potential. It is the detail that made me realize the power of teamwork and I have been focused on team-building since 2013.

The plan works when you work the plan.

You would imagine everything went well from there and the obstacles were over?

Think again.

I was working on the gold project for a few months when the compliance office told me that my use of my company name in a domain name was not permitted. This caused me to lose most of my work.

Then I switched my focus and started building with a Bitcoin company where I had no restrictions on my creativity and it took only about six months to achieve my financial independence.

I was on a run. I wanted the financial freedom, too, so I started working with a travel company, but after months of developing tools and campaigns, I received an email from the compliance office and it killed that dream on the spot. It seemed like it was time to get out of my comfort zone, so I backed off on network marketing, working part-time while I went back to school.

Because I was aware I was an amateur in my trading

activities, I found a mentor and took a course to learn to read charts, crypto-currencies, stocks, and commodities. I started trading like a pro and that is how I made my first million dollars—by focusing 15 hours a day, with no days off, for about two years.

I used this opportunity to update my dream list and relocate to Thailand, where I still reside today. Ironically, the travel company I placed on stand-by has plans to open their business in Thailand, and I now plan to go back into travel mode and network marketing full-time soon.

Since then, I also found a way to work with multiple companies without creating compliance issues.

Some things I have learned on my journey:

- In the networking industry, who you join is more important than what you join.
- Surround yourself with people who empower you to be your best self.
- Most people are focusing on the wrong "m" (money vs. mindset).
- Do not worry about what other people think, say, or do.
- Multiple streams of income are no longer a luxury. They are a necessity.

The following affirmations have worked well for me, and I am happy to share them with you. The first one led me to wonderful things, events, and people, and started changing my "to-do's" to "done:"

- "I now command my subconscious mind to guide me in the right direction, to commit the right actions, and find the right people to help me reach all of my goals and objectives, right now."

The next one is my "X2" affirmation. I was earning an average of $10,000/month when I decided to X2 it. I focused on this affirmation and I eventually got it.

- 2X: "I am a Gold Director Elite (GDE) earning more than $24,000 per month."
(*GDE is the highest rank one can reach within the gold company compensation plan.)

First, it was a thought in my mind before becoming a reality in my life. It may seem too simple, but the truth is that visualization really does work when you add feelings to it.

Once I understood how easy it was to double my income, I started on the X4 affirmation.

- 4X: "I am a GDE earning more than $24,000 per WEEK."

One day, I realized I made more than $100,000 in a month, but that was the easy part. The real challenge is in doing it again and again, so then I switched my focus to a 7-figure mindset.

- 10X: "I have a millionaire mind and a millionaire lifestyle. I also have a million dollars in the bank and many millions worth of gold and Bitcoin. Most importantly, I am in position to improve the life of millions of people and that's exactly what I'm doing while I enjoy every minute of it."

It is only when I started to focus on a millionaire mindset that I realized I had a limiting belief and was thinking step-by-step, so I decided to skip a step and go directly from six to eight figures. By asking myself the question, *"How can I make more than $1 million per month?"* I found the way to do it.

What about you?

Have you ever thought of transforming your annual income into your monthly income?

If I did it, you can do it too. What the mind can conceive and feel, the mind can achieve.

Sadly, 90% of people are still not aware of the habits, patterns, and paradigms that prevent them from starting to live on their own terms.

I like helping people reach their dreams. Feel free to connect with me at any time. I answer everyone who takes the time to send me a message.

Thank you for taking the time to read about my break through!

Biography

Steven Bourgeois is a 48-year-old French Canadian who has been living in Vietnam and Thailand since 2006. Still single with no children, he is aware of the value of education for children and aspires to transform this passion into a full-time fulfillment lifestyle.

A pioneer of the internet from the early 1990s, Steven strongly believes that, "Science and technology coupled with people of good will is one way to solve hunger and poverty worldwide." He is working to prove his theory.

World traveler, network marketer, trader, investor, and team builder, Steven also believes mindset is crucial and the most important thing to consider in life to live our passions fully. He loves sharing knowledge and meeting new people.

Contact Information:

Web: http://7plusteam.com
Email: 7plusteam@gmail.com

Chapter Fifteen

Unlock Your Greatness

Vernae Taylor

From the moment I had eyes, I liked boys and I craved their attention.

I *always* had a boyfriend. Always! There was puppy love Jeffrey in grade school. There was Kevin in high school and going into college. There was Frank, who loved me fiercely (but was super possessive, jealous and controlling). Then there was Anthony (who sort of rescued me from Frank).

Sadly, Anthony was everything I wanted and needed, but I was too damaged to recognize it. I was confrontational, insecure, broken, and battered.

I had been bounced around since I was in diapers. There was a time my older brother and I lived with our parents. But (as I have been told) there were so many times we were left with friends of the family or with my grandmother. At some point, I was with one of my aunts on my mother's side, and it was not long before she dropped me off at my grandmother's house and said, "I can't keep her."

From that moment on, when I was a toddler and my brother was about 6-7 years old, my grandmother went through the process of fighting for full custody of us. She always said that she didn't want us to be separated and she definitely didn't want us to be in foster care.

My grandmother is everything to me! She is the matriarch of our family and is still bouncing around, even at her mature age. She works one day a week at the church, and the entire community loves her. She is a sharp-witted, small southern lady with such wisdom and strength. She has outlived husbands, buried two sons, and reared my brother and me. She even worked three jobs at once just to make sure ends would meet. We always had three meals, clothes ironed, nice things, and never felt left out of the crowd with activities and sports. She did all of it without having a driver's license no less.

My grandmother represents stability to me, even to this very day. Her phone number is unchanged and she still lives in the apartment she lived in after migrating from North Carolina to New Jersey, when her rent was only $75 per month. She loves Tyler Perry movies (that part always makes me smile), doing her own grocery shopping, and she is the oldest living resident in Summit, New Jersey, and refuses to move into an assisted living home. She is and will always be one of my heroes.

My dad was a "cool cat." He was a skilled carpenter who could fix virtually anything. A poet and a lover of progressive jazz, he walked around the neighborhood spreading wisdom and light to the younger generation. He was always physically present for my brother and me, but had a vice or two that robbed him of the capacity to be there emotionally and financially, and it controlled him. There were times he tried to live on his own, but my grandmother did not want him to be homeless or to be out on the street in a drunken state for the world to see.

In addition to all the confusion, addiction, alcoholism, and overbearing nature of the family, I have been told that my mother had a breakdown. She never felt like her efforts to be there for us was good enough. I guess you could say she reached her limit, threw her hands up, and stepped back from it all. However, no matter where she was; be it in a hospital, shelter, homeless, or otherwise, she always visited, wrote letters, sent handmade birthday cards, called, and did what she could.

At times, I resented the fact that she had to bounce around from house to house or shelter to shelter, while my dad, even in the depths of his substance abuse, was able to live somewhat of a "good life."

My resentment eventually caused a strain on my relationship with my father, and I was no longer a "daddy's girl." As a teenager, I grew angry, combative, and very vocal about my hatred toward him. (It sounds harsh even replaying it in my mind). I felt emotionally abandoned by him, and was sure it was his fault that my mother was gone. I often felt misunderstood by family and friends and every bit of my life was a fight.

Naturally, it would have been a challenge to have both my mom and dad under the same roof with my grandmother, because my parents were in fact divorced. In my mind, it seemed like we were living in a house on the hill, secured by a great big fence. My mother was on the wrong side of that fence as an outsider, and ostracized and rejected by her own family and it seemed as if her side of the family offered little to no support through it all.

I was a troubled, angry teen. I had a horrible temper and after negative patterns that played out in my relationships, I knew I had to make a change. As I started to uncover the truth of my past, I gained a stronger desire to want to rewrite it and not repeat it.

My mother resides in New Jersey with her husband of 15-plus years. She and I are extremely close and we speak frequently. She has revealed to me a lot of things that I did not know about our family history. She answers every question I have. But in a moment of self-realization, I had to admit to her that I am still working through my issues of abandonment and resentment. She still feels horrible at times for what she and my father put us through.

I have forgiven her, yet my soul and spirit have not forgotten. To this day, I believe the breakdown of our family has played a role in my reluctance to have children or get married.

Only more time, prayer, healing, and soul searching will tell what the future holds. I remind my mother as often as I can that I am not giving up and will keep on fighting for my life, my dreams, and to unlock my purpose, while inspiring others to do the same.

For a time, I lived with my aunt, my dad's sister, who was extremely influential in my upbringing. We were having a heated argument, as we often had. Now let me just go back and paint a picture of how explosive my temper could be sometimes. As a child, I witnessed the anger my brother felt, and I would act out as well, by screaming, crying, throwing things, and slamming doors. On one occasion, my aunt and I were having a heated debate, and at some point I became so enraged that I nearly lost control of my body.

When I happened to pass by a mirror, I saw my reflection, and I was terrified! I did not recognize that person. I was shaking uncontrollably and it felt like an out-of-body experience. I remember the feeling of urgency to get out of there quick. I ran outside to my car and jumped in and sped off as fast as I could. I thank God for his safety, even in my moment of ruin. I remember my girlfriend mentioning a Mental Health Center and how many great resources they had there. It was on that same day that I checked myself in and asked to be evaluated right away. I shared the episode of rage with the lady and told her that I needed help before I hurt myself or somebody else. That was day one of therapy. I continued therapy out of that facility for many, many years. It is an ongoing process of accountability.

Anthony was everything I wanted—or so I thought. He was there for me when I had to get a protective order against Frank. He listened to the stories of the time I locked myself in my dorm room in fear of Frank's aggression and control. I was not in a position to be vulnerable, to be loved, or to receive it. I sabotaged our possible relationship from the beginning. Completely unwilling to compromise or grow, I stepped on his manhood and pushed him away. Suddenly, there was a shift in our dynamic. He had the upper hand and he began to make me feel as if I was not enough and never would be.

Let's face it, I was emotionally unstable. I did not know how to communicate strong emotions without yelling and unfairly hitting below the belt with my words and insults. I was ruthless and reckless. Anthony knew it, saw my weakness, and began to belittle me. He knew that I hung on his every word. If he wanted my hair short, I did it. If he noticed my nails were getting too long, I would cut them. He would say, "I don't like no skinny girls" so I would get thicker. But I had to be careful, because if I gained too much weight, he would notice that too.

The relationship was over in his mind. Yet, it lingered on for years. He knew I couldn't be his "happily ever after" in my current state. We sought counseling, mentoring, and prayer. I was lost in him and had no identity. I depended on Anthony to make me happy and fix what was broken, and he could not and should not have assumed such an incredible task. I wanted to save the relationship because he was "my everything." But I could not even save myself. He did not grow up in dysfunction and discord. He had both parents and somehow, they never raised their voices and knew how to manage their emotions. Anything else was foreign and lethal to him and he rejected all interruptions to his peace.

Everything came full circle once I turned 30, with the demise of a long-term relationship, and the resurgence of a bond with my father. Then, all too soon, my father was quickly yanked from my life again and forever. I was left feeling defeated once more, because I could not get my dad sober, I could not cure cancer, and I could not make Anthony stay and love me back to life. Neither one of them chose me. Once again, I felt worthless, hopeless, and lost.

Now for the first time, I had to become my *own* hero. I could no longer blame my mother for the time that she missed with me, my father for not being able to beat his addiction, or my brother not being able to save me because he was pursuing his own healing. Just like when I walked past the mirror and caught a glimpse of who was reflected back at me, I had to understand that I might have been at least part of my problem up until this point.

But I am also my solution.

First, I had to get to a place of quietness and solitude. I am not capable of reconciling all the wrongs in my family or my upbringing and I had to first accept that. It was up to me to build my own confidence and self-worth. They say a father is supposed to do that, that he builds the self-esteem in his daughter. He is supposed to be the first man to take her out on a date; the first man to say "I love you" and share secrets with her; be there to catch her whenever she falls; and protect her from unnecessary hurt and pain. I knew my father loved me and he made time to say it, but he did not make me a priority or foster a sense of security in me.

So, I am left here to figure it all out. I began my healing by asking myself, "Who am I?" I am a woman—a woman who needs affection, to be affirmed, and to feel safe. I realized in the very moment that I asked the question, that this had to begin with *me*. I had to be kind to myself. I vividly remember when my therapist challenged me by saying, "Would you ever speak to your best friend as cruelly as you speak to yourself?"

In order to drown out the negative voices in my head, I had to replace them with something positive and noble, so I practiced speaking to myself with words of love and encouragement. Yes, I was *that* girl with sticky notes all over my vanity, the one flooding her cell phone calendar with quotes and scriptures.

Sometimes, it was not enough to quietly read these things to myself. Instead, I had to recite them out loud, whether I was in my car, at home, or at work. I had to repeat the words over and over again and use them as weapons against my own doubt, defeat, and self-destruction. I had to be reminded that "I'm worthy, simply because I was born." I believe I heard Oprah or Maya Angelou say it first, but they were right and I needed to start believing it!

I did nice things for myself. You know as a "serial relationship queen," I never knew what it felt like to take myself to dinner, a movie, or to enjoy a pampering day that was planned by me, for me. I never thought I would have the courage to do it.

My happiness and my being whole will be solely up to me from this second forward. I had to crack open all those books that people had given to me that I had not been brave enough to read, books like *Beauty for Ashes, Turning Hurts into Halos, The Power of Now, Mandela's Way: Lessons on Life, Love and Courage,* and the good old *Holy Bible*, to name a few.

And, I had to let go of the guilt and shame from my past and give myself permission to tell my story. "Whatever it takes for my own sanity and emotional freedom" is what I often tell myself. I'm committed to renewing myself daily; and writing my feelings down, no matter how embarrassing or horrifying. I practice gratitude by recording every single success and good event of the day, no matter how great or small, and I became intentional and specific with every prayer.

I built up the strength to eliminate the noise, the naysayers, and the toxic people and relationships, and started to get real with what and who I wanted to be. I was afraid of my own greatness, I suppose. Let's face it, in order to be great, we must one day be weak. In order to obtain success, we had to fail one day, but most of us resist the valleys and the lows.

As I searched in the deepest, darkest parts of my mind, heart, and soul, I found myself there and had to be reborn. I had to let my old habits die, and dispose of false ideologies of myself and how the world was to be around me. I would say the greatest challenge of them all was that I had to surrender *all* control of how people were to treat me or show up in my life. I had to set the tone by cultivating positive energy, learning how to retain and harness that same energy and project it out into the world (first). I needed to set the tone of what love should look like by loving and respecting myself (first). I had to revisit old hobbies that used to bring me joy and laughter and be deliberate about enjoying life again.

When you self-reflect and search for answers to your problems from the inside out, that is where you will meet your own humanity—you confront honesty, acceptance, forgiveness, and patience—and it all begins with *you*.

Be honest with whoever you are discovering yourself to be right now, even in the frazzled state in which you find yourself. *Accept full responsibility* of the journey it will take to become something new and *forgive yourself* for mistakes made, poor choices, and regret. Lastly, *be patient* because no real transformation happens overnight.

The work of soul searching became a major key in my healing and will one day become the catalyst for my success.

Just remember, a breakthrough is not finite and it does not always take on a singular path. A breakthrough is not immediate and it is not always a one-time assignment. It is something that we are constantly having to do, because life is going to bring us numerous occasions in which we are going to have to pick ourselves up, dust ourselves off, and keep moving forward in another direction, consciously making a different choice, and falling to our knees pleading for God's help.

There will be times when we are going to cry out and wish it were all over. Train to fight those moments!

Let me leave you with this: It is not a breakthrough, rather it is *I am breaking through.* I have been breaking through and I hope you do, too.

Biography

Author, singer, actress, and host Vernae Taylor is on a mission to help people achieve greatness and live every day with purpose.

She is a proud alumna of Rutgers University and has publicly spoken on bridging the gap among sectors within organizations, the impact of performing arts within society, and the influence of elders within the community.

As the founder of Triple Threat Vision, an events company, she has hosted a Sister-to-Sister "Talk Back" and *The Family Affair: A Collective Arts Experience*, creating a platform for entrepreneurs and talents within a family friendly atmosphere. Her planned future projects include a live podcast in Winter 2019, publishing her first volume of poetry: *LIFE, LOVE, LOSS*, and a book in her father's memory, *Letters to my Father*.

Contact Information:

Triple Threat Vision, LLC
P. O. Box 235
Summit, NJ 07902

www.vernae.com
Email: triplethreatvisionllc@gmail.com
Facebook: @vernaetaylor
Facebook: @triplethreatvision
Instagram: @vernaetaylor

CHAPTER SIXTEEN

Born to be B.A.D.

Mike Williams

Very rarely will you hear someone suggest that the best variable for success is being *bad*, but that's exactly what I'm suggesting to you. Once you take a few minutes and read the following chapter, I'm sure you'll agree that the system I share and have established in my own life is the most beneficial set of beliefs you can adopt in your pursuit of success.

I established these principles on my journey in becoming an NCAA national champion wrestler, but whether you are an athlete, entrepreneur, corporate leader, or just desire to finish a job you've set out to do, they'll work for you as well.

So, why *bad*, you ask? It sounds counterintuitive, as we are taught to be *good* from the time we started walking and talking. Don't worry, I'm not advocating for you to break any laws, or rob a bank. *BAD* (or B.A.D.) is an acronym, with each letter representing a necessary component of the success formula.

Before we jump right in, I must disclose that though B.A.D. is my proprietary system, the individual components are not a new methodology, but rather simple and highly effective elements of success, proven to help strengthen your overall focus, accountability, and results.

The first component of B.A.D. is *Belief.*

Why belief? Rarely has greatness been achieved without unmeasurable faith throughout the journey.

Belief is a state or habit of mind in which trust or confidence is placed in something or someone.

It has been said that the strongest factor for success is self-esteem: *believing you can do it, believing you deserve it,* and *believing you'll get it.* We all have a belief system, and it determines many of our endeavors in life as well as our views of ourselves and others.

You probably know several people with a very fragile belief system. Since they're uncertain about their own values, it's easy for their thoughts and actions to be influenced by the outside world, the people around them, and, unfortunately their own negative internal monologue.

Then, you know those who have a very solid and unshakable belief system. Even during adversity, conflict, or uncertainty, they stand true on what they believe, and their belief system allows them to commit wholeheartedly to a solution or desired goal.

As an All-American two years in a row, by the start of the 2011 wrestling season I wanted nothing more than to become an NCAA national champion and stand atop that podium. I had started wrestling when I was four years old in the wrestling hotbed of central New Jersey, and I had yet to win a national title. Though I began the 2011 season ranked in the top five nationally in my weight class, I began having doubts about my ability to become a national champion.

The season started off in sour defeat: one win, one loss, and an injury that caused me to forfeit the remainder of a tournament. However, that injury resulted in a new beginning for me because during that time something remarkable happened as I spent time in recovery. I finally began to believe in my own ability, and I promised myself: *I will* not *lose again for the rest of the season.*

Roy T. Bennett, author of *The Light in the Heart*, wrote, "Believe in your infinite potential. Your only limitations are those you set upon yourself."

I agree with Bennett. If you aim to be successful, you must develop *belief.*

While forming my B.A.D. principles, I've found three ideals to be essential in developing belief:

- *Consistent effort compounded over time (repetition) creates massive results*
- *Measurable progress within a reasonable time frame*
- *Competence or mastery of skill*

My wrestling career up to that point had been a marathon, not a sprint, and it was through the first ideal of consistent effort over time that I developed my skills. I endured years of defeats, long practices, and disappointments prior to winning a high school state title or NCAA national title. Consistent effort over time doesn't only help you build *belief*, it develops character, grit, and discipline.

One of my favorite quotes is from Orrin Woodward, "There are many shortcuts to failure, but there are no shortcuts to true success."

The second ideal, *measurable progress within a reasonable timeframe*, is quite different than *consistent effort over time*, but both coincide. Making measurable progress within a reasonable timeframe will require you to put forth consistent effort. The key with this concept is defining a *reasonable timeframe* because it will vary from task to task. Learning a new function in your profession may take significantly less time than building a multimillion-dollar firm. So, it is important to identify how you are measuring progress and what timeframe is practical and in alignment with the goal you are pursuing.

Your consistent effort and your progress segue into the last ideal in developing belief, *competence and mastery of skill*. You should aim to become the go-to person, the subject matter expert in your sport, business, or field of study. If you have ever watched Michael Jordan in his prime, a doctor diagnosing an illness, or a classically trained musician playing an instrument, chances are their powerful skills and deep belief in their own competence were honed by much repetition and constant improvement.

The A in B.A.D. is *Action*, and it's the heart of belief. Hold that thought; we'll come back to action after we discuss what's behind D—*Desire*.

What's desire? It's defined as a strong feeling of wanting to have something or wishing for something to happen, and it's the one thing I can't help you develop. Desire is not a habit; it's not an ideal or philosophy. It's not even a tactic. Desire is intrinsic. It's shaped by who you are and what you value.

Desire requires you to look inward and really find what drives you. Start by really pinpointing your *why*, the thing that drives you beyond yourself whenever you want to throw in the towel or lose focus on your dreams. Your *why* is the thing that keeps you grounded and gets you back on track.

Once you have your *why* and determine what it is you desire, you must then realize this one truth in pursuing a BAD mindset: *Your desire can outweigh your belief, but your belief can never outweigh your desire.* This concept can be further proven by the myriad of people whom you know who are extremely talented at something but fail to commit to it for the long haul.

They never will become highly successful at their talent, but if you ask them, "Why haven't you been more successful at X?" They will most likely give you some trite response if they are like most people.

The question then becomes, *Why haven't they, truly?* Yes, there can be factors such as luck or timing. Still, there's one common truth: Without desire, it is difficult to maximize potential, no matter how talented you are. Life is an equal opportunity employer when it comes to adversity, and if you only deliver results based on talent, and lack desire and will, you will be a mere fraction of your best and most optimal self.

In the 2011-2012 wrestling season, *desire* was what I had going for me on my quest to become a national champion, long before I had articulated my B.A.D. philosophy or even considered it to be a success system. Desire drove me to be consistent in my effort. Desire drove me to do an extra workout, and manage my weight, despite my love for McDonald's fries.

Even when you have great talent, mastery of skill, and overwhelming belief, without the *desire* to reach any goal of significance, you will likely fall short when you meet the right level of adversity.

How do I know, you ask?

Your adversity could be the loss of a job or a loved one, weight gain, social pressures, any bump in your path that could deter you from committing to the long and uncertain journey toward success. Without a desire for the task, goal, or skill that you are pursuing, the chances are you'll succumb to the constant pressures within you to take the safe route.

Desire inspires courage. So how do we look inward and ask the right questions? Here are specific questions you can ask to get the wheels turning.

- If money is no longer a factor, what will you do in life?
- Do you believe the goal you're pursuing is a worthy goal?
- Do your actions align with your true desire?

The answers to these questions will only lead to more questions. Really hone in on your answers, and you can examine your true desires, shift your behavior, and transform your life.

Before we move to what I believe is the most important component in B.A.D, you should recognize while each of these components represents a concept, before they can yield great measures of success, they require synergy and simultaneous execution.

The *A* in B.A.D. stands for *Action*—the glue for *Belief* and *Desire*.

BELIEF ⟵⟶ *ACTION* ⟵⟶ *DESIRE*

I sat in the crowd, listening to a distinguished speaker delivering the keynote speech to a major business conference as he analyzed several principles on leadership, sales tips, and life success, he said, "The largest gap in the world is the gap between knowledge and application, the gap between knowing and doing."

He made it clear that action (or application of knowledge) is critical. Unlike the emotional drivers of belief and desire, action is a tangible act and one that creates habits.

Taking action can be quite difficult for a number of reasons. Persistence is the willingness to be knocked down, rejected, not get the result you longed for or as quickly as you anticipated, and yet get back up on the horse with a laser focus. A lack of persistence is a main reason people stop acting or applying themselves.

Here's my first B.A.D. challenge: Choose your most important goal, and during the next 30 days, I challenge you to be persistent enough to deal with the tough times and to get to the light at the end of the tunnel, whatever your goal may be.

Let's go back to my mediocre 1-1 opening tournament in 2011. After my injury, I rallied off 33 straight wins during the remainder of the season and finished with a 34-1 record. Persistence allowed me to look beyond one poor performance and gave me the fortitude in several close matches that were decided by two points or less.

I succeeded in reaching my goal in March 2012, when I became the Division II 165-pound NCAA National Wrestling Champion.

To be successful, you must be persistent.

Next, is the art of discipline. A lack of discipline will cause you to be inconsistent with your actions. The type of discipline I'm talking about can be described by the simple phrase, "Do what you need to, not what you want to."

This phrase was repeated all the time by my college wrestling coach, Jamie Gibbs. When I was an 18-year-old kid, I didn't put much thought into it and considered his words on discipline just some cliché motto. Over time, I realized what he meant as I watched the guys on the team. The more seasoned and disciplined athletes trained, studied, and maintained a well-balanced social life.

Those guys had a much greater probability of being successful in all realms of their lives. Discipline is a powerful component; with it, you can do anything (in time); without it, you wonder where time went!

For my second B.A.D. challenge, I challenge you to be disciplined during the next 30 days. "Do what you need to do, not what you want to do." If it's quitting a bad habit, be disciplined enough to change and manage your habits. If it's becoming healthier, be disciplined enough to carve out the time to exercise. If it's improving your leadership, be disciplined enough to seek out feedback from trusted advisors, make the adjustments, and maintain those behaviors moving forward.

To be successful and take consistent action, you must be disciplined.

One of the most common reasons people fail to act is analysis paralysis, or waiting until the perfect moment, perfect solution, or perfect circumstances to move forward with an idea. Of course, this ultimately leads to no decision being made at all. This behavior is typical in perfectionists.

When does perfection exist? Hardly ever. Unfortunately, many high achievers suffer from analysis paralysis because of self-inflicted stress, unrealistic expectations, or self-imposed pressure. Overthinking can stifle your creativity, create barriers to achieving results, and make you less happy.

So, how do you improve? The founder of Dropbox, billionaire Drew Houston, said a deceptively simple thing that I'll never forget: "If you have a dream, you can spend a lifetime studying, planning, and getting ready for it. What you *should* be doing is getting *started."*

Next, change your perspective from a *could* to a *must*. When ideas, goals, and aspirations become *must*, you will intuitively remove obstacles, take risks, and be more committed to the result than if you were just pursuing something that's a "could". There's a psychological, emotional, and personal difference in saying you *could* accomplish something, and you *must* accomplish it. A *must* propels you to act, a *could* gives you the option to move or not move.

Before I finally became an NCAA national champion, I decided that I *must* win. I didn't take any shortcuts and went far past the minimum work expected of me. Some weekends, I completely sacrificed my social life to commit to the process of becoming a national champion. In my mind, I worked too hard not to win. Before I boarded the plane to the tournament, I said, "I must win!" and I believed it. Develop a *must* mindset!

An important element of the *action* concept is timeliness. Far too many people live as though they have infinite time here on Earth. It is critical to set a deadline for your goals and ask someone you trust to hold you accountable. You'll find that you achieve more, are more productive, and you'll become B.A.D. in the process.

Time is free, but it's priceless. You can't own it, but you can use it. You can't keep it, but you can spend it. Once you've lost it you can never get it back.

—Harvey Mackay

My final 30-day-challenge is for you to stop researching, planning, and overthinking the goal that's been on your list for the last year or more. Instead, take *action*.

Let's tie this all together: Combine *belief, action, and desire*, and that's when you'll be B.A.D. Being B.A.D. enables you to become a more effective influencer, leader, high performer, and overall success in whatever endeavor you decide to pursue.

My hope for you is that you implement these concepts immediately. I guarantee you'll radically and positively change your life and the lives of those around you, just as my life has been changed.

Now go be B.A.D.!

Biography

Speaker, entrepreneur, and NCAA national champion wrestler Mike Williams grew up in Plainfield, New Jersey, in a neighborhood plagued with violence, drugs, and broken families. By the time he was 13, he had gang ties; he became a father by 17, and lost his twin sister to gun violence at age 22.

With the drive and determination to be successful, Mike was able to overcome the obstacles that claimed so many young men in his neighborhood. Mike graduated with a BA in Criminal Justice degree from UNC-Pembroke, where he also became a member of Omega Psi Phi Fraternity Inc. He has a Master Certificate in Supply Chain Management and Operations from Michigan State University and is completing his MBA at Louisiana State University at Shreveport. He is a Senior Operations Manager for a Fortune 500 company.

Mike has been speaking on self-development, leadership, and business success for years in different forums, focusing on high school and college students. Mike, his wife, Charis Williams, and their family reside in the Charlotte, N.C., area. He has two sons, Samaj and Mahki, and two daughters, Lyric and Milli-Grace. His hobbies include collecting international banknotes, traveling, and MMA.

Contact information

Website: mikewilliamsspeaks.com
Email: mikewilliams@mwspeaks.com
Facebook: Mike Williams (@MikeWilliamsMission180)
Instagram: MikeWilliamsmission180

CHAPTER SEVENTEEN

Go for Confidence

Wojciech Mach

Growing up, I was tremendously skinny and quite tall. The combination did not give me a healthy, slim, and trim look. It was more the starving refugee look.

I really stood out in a crowd of children, and everyone noticed how bony I was. The children at school said a lot of things to me about my weight, and none of the things they said were nice.

There was no medical reason for my weight issue. It was a matter of genetics and biology.

"Some people are just skinny," the doctor said.

We tried some protein shakes and other dietary changes to help me put on weight with no success. I tried working out to bulk up and build up my body mass without a lot of success.

My mother suffered from the same insecurity when she was young and she was extremely skinny as well. With her help, my insecurity became a multi-generational belief that there was something wrong with me. In her way, my mother was trying to protect me and make me feel better. Because of how insecure she felt herself, instead she actually helped pile more anxiety onto the anxiety I already felt.

When I was a teenager at summer camp, one event happened that I remember exceptionally well because it shaped me for a long time. A mixed crowd of boys and girls were playing volleyball when this happened, and I was trying to smash the ball. When I completely missed my smash, one girl pointed to my legs and made fun of how skinny they were. In front of everyone, she blamed my legs for why I could not hit the volleyball.

Her words reinforced what was already in my head—that I did not measure up with others physically.

At that time in my young life, it felt very important to me that I find acceptance from others, particularly from young women. I wanted to look good in front of the girls I liked. It was humiliating to be called out like that and to be the object of ridicule. Because of her words, I made the decision to not show how I looked from then on. I tried to cover my embarrassment by wearing long shorts.

Adversity in our lives causes some people to become stronger and it causes some people to break. I allowed that girl's opinion to dictate how I felt about myself. I allowed her comments to take away my confidence and dictate my reality. It affected my personal confidence and how I approached people for a very long time. I tried acting like something I was not to fit into the expectations that society had of me.

This pattern continued for more than ten years. I was depressed, and running on low self-esteem. Ironically, I felt as if the weight of the world was on my shoulders.

I grew up after the collapse of communism in Eastern Europe and the post-democratic era started. It was a time when there were not a lot of things for sale on store shelves. Even things like oranges and sweets were rare treats. My parents both were well educated and belonged to the middle class. My Dad was a French teacher. My mom worked as an engineer.

I was the third of four children in our family. My siblings were very high achievers in school while I was not. I was an okay student, just not stellar. To get the attention from my parents that I always needed and wanted, I used negative behavior. I was punished at home, of course. My parents hoped I would meet their expectations and be good, but I could not.

The problem was not lack of effort on my part. Throughout middle school and high school, I was always approaching girls, but usually after a certain point in any kind of relationship or friendship, they backed off. I was becoming very desperate and needy. I had a pattern of falling in love quickly, and usually my girlfriends left me equally quickly without saying why. As a result, I was getting more and more frustrated.

When you combine my behavior with my awkward skinny body, one that just kept growing taller and taller, and don't include healthy coping skills we develop as adults, you can see why I felt terrible and frustrated all the time. I was just filled with frustration up until I went to university. There I found substitutes for relationships, like alcohol and other stupid activities, and they did not help me feel better about myself.

I do not think I am that unique. How many of you have found yourselves victims of the opinions of others? How long did what other people say dictate your reality? In my case, not only did it affect my personal confidence, it affected how I approached women for a very long time. And there is another aspect of this for both men and women: We allow our perception of how we look, how our bodies look, to be dictated by society and that is completely wrong.

My journey was a long process. It didn't take just one area of self-improvement for me to outgrow this self-destructive behavior. It takes time.

This did not happen overnight.

What helped me was when I began to learn about relationships. I got in with an online community of men who wanted to improve their relationships and increase their self-confidence. Becoming part of that community also was helpful.

My breakthrough finally came when I stopped listening to the opinions of others and embraced my own story; I didn't continue my path of looking for stories about other people and molding them to fit me. We *all* need to find our own stories.

The key to my breakthrough was taking a 21-day challenge course. The course was designed to gain self-confidence in relationships.

It was a go-and-do type of self-progressive course. On the eighteenth day, I experienced a breakthrough which removed the weight on my shoulders for once and for all. The course taught about the whole process of attraction and interaction. I learned to become more sociable overall, with both men and women, and learned to understand the dynamics between people. It's true: The more you talk to people, the better at it you become.

The course was a game-changer for me. I felt my self-confidence return in all areas of my life.

The course I took is no longer available online, so I took

the basic ideas, added my own variations and insights, and adapted ideas from others to create a new 20-day challenge—titled *Go For Confidence*—to help all people improve their self-image. The course is available on my website, listed at the end of the chapter. It is a self-directed course; you do not move on to the next challenge until you complete your assignment. Conceivably, the course could take you more than 20 days, if you work slowly.

This course will help you get a lot of wrong ideas out of your head, and it will help you no matter what your individual goal is. My goal was to meet my soul mate, a dream woman who represented all the personality traits I was seeking. And I found her. We now have been married for three years. Our first child, a daughter, is four months old.

When I met my wife, it was on a dancers' holiday in Tunisia—a vacation just for people who enjoy salsa dancing. More than 100 people were on this holiday. When I started speaking with her, I easily understood her social cues. I instantly had a lot of confidence with her. She was still living in Poland while I had moved to the UK. It was a long-distance relationship for a while and then she moved to the UK and marriage followed. It is a dream come true for me.

Go For Confidence will help you to remove a lot of negative ideas from your head. Obviously, it is a very deep kind of challenge. Each person taking the course might have a different goal.

The people with whom I have shared the course have had great successes in what they hoped to accomplish. I shared some of the course with my younger brother and it helped him. He was going through some of the same difficulties I had faced and along the way he discovered himself. He also met the woman who later became his wife.

The world is a different place now. There are thousands of people who meet every day through online dating. Everything is completely different than it was ten, twenty, or thirty years ago. People do not have the same opportunities for meeting others and socializing. That is why *Go For Confidence* can benefit so many people.

In whatever we do in life, sometimes we limit ourselves and do not reach for the golden ring when we should. This course will help you learn how to do it.

Creating *Go For Confidence* also helped me realize how I can help my daughter to never be affected by the same type of thinking I was as a child and teenager, no matter what she looks like.

First, I do not have the body image issues anymore, so that is not something I will be passing on to her. I am still a very skinny, very tall guy, but I believe it is to my advantage and not a fault. I am not worried about it. I will teach my daughter that whatever she looks like, she is perfect. I may share my story: I was skinny and tall, and it all turned out fine.

I will tell my daughter that I will love her the way she is. She will feel very strongly loved and supported all the time. Life will give us examples. I do not believe we can protect kids from everything that is bad or negative in the world, but I believe we can give them coping mechanisms so that when they are faced with something, they can deal with it.

Developing *Go For Confidence* also helped me realize there are things I need to do to keep my relationship with my wife strong and growing.

Five Steps to Building a Better Relationship

1. *Know yourself and know your strengths.* You must know who you really are, otherwise no one else can know you, either.
2. *Have a common vision of the relationship partnership.* Know the expectations of each party in the relationship.
3. *Open communication.* Something men are not always good at is communication. Many of us did not have good examples to follow when we were growing up. *Go For Confidence* can help with that.
4. *Learn to apologize and do it often.* My wife and I have strong personalities. Sometimes we have differing opinions, different points of view. We learn to forgive and accept some of the other person's beliefs. You must find common ground sometimes.
5. *Make God a part of your lives together.* Marriage is not just a relationship with someone; it's a relationship with God as well. I believe this can save us. When we commit to one person, we must make sure God is part of the long-term plan.

I believe my story and course can help others who have problems with self-confidence. Youths are bombarded with pictures about body image and it is damaging.

I would love to help other people with this breakthrough if they are going through the same issues I faced—insecurities, communication difficulties, and a lack of self-confidence.

I tell you with all that's in my heart: Go out and have an amazing life!

Biography

Wojciech Mach was born in Poland and moved to the United Kingdom in 2008. Now 38 years old, he lives with his wife, Joanna, and daughter, Maya, in the east suburbs of London.

Wojciech earned a degree in mechanical engineering from AGH Cracow University of Technology. He participated in a student exchange program in France, which included an internship. His postgraduate studies were in project management.

Although an engineer by profession, Wojciech has discovered another passion—networking. He is a passionate network marketer, and he enjoys helping others by making relevant introductions that benefit both individuals and businesses.

His hobbies include Cuban music and salsa dancing, traveling, personal development, and networking.

Go For Confidence is available free to readers of this book. Enter the code "BREAKTHROUGH" to receive the course at no charge.

Wojciech requests that people who use the course leave a comment or feedback after completing the challenge to help others.

Contact Information:

www.wojciechmach.com
Email: info@wojciechmach.com

CHAPTER EIGHTEEN

Escape the Ordinary

Nik Halik

As a child, you used to dream. Your mind wasn't shackled by logic, false beliefs, or societal limitations. Everything was possible, and the world was wondrous and magical. Then, as you aged, you started developing false and limiting beliefs about yourself and the world around you. You started buying into societal programming. When people told you something wasn't possible, you believed them. When your peers chose jobs and careers based on their own internal limitations, you followed suit. You started thinking more "responsibly" and "sensibly." And in this process, the flame of your dreams died down to mere embers, and in some cases may have been entirely extinguished.

My invitation to you is to breathe life into your dreams again. Cast off the shackles of your false beliefs and societal programming. Realize the vast majority of your limitations are only in your mind.

What would you do if money was no longer the primary reason for doing or not doing something? What grand adventures would you live? What noble causes would you champion? What great feats would you accomplish?

179

I was born with a poor biological template. I developed chronic allergies, debilitating asthma, and I was nearsighted. I was medically confined to my bedroom for the first decade of my life. When I was eight years old, a traveling salesman knocked on our front door in Port Melbourne, Australia, and sold my non-English speaking Greek immigrant parents a set of the Encyclopedia Britannica. That set turned out to be one of the greatest influences on my life. It was the spark and secret kindling that set my imagination on fire. My imagination had stretched my mind, and it would never retract to its original dimensions.

I read the encyclopedia constantly and, without my parents knowing, I'd take it to bed with me. I'd shine a flashlight under the sheets, flick the pages of a volume through to a subject that fascinated me, and read until I nodded off to sleep. Sometimes I'd stay awake past midnight, dreaming about the things I was going to pursue in life, and imagining the world that was out there waiting for me.

Growing up, an inspirational character for me was the comic book adventurer named Tintin. Tintin was living the "never grow up" dream, and I traveled the world through his pages, taking in every exotic detail. I read and reread Tintin books in our school library, daydreaming about his magical life. In his various adventures he was a pilot, space explorer, mountain climber, and deep-sea diver. He also climbed the mountains of Nepal, rescued African slaves, battled pirates, and dived down to the deepest abyss of the ocean to explore shipwrecks.

When I reflect on the adventures of Tintin, I realize my

childhood dreams have come true. Many times, in the course of my adventures, I've been in some far-flung destination and had a weird feeling of déjà vu—a Tintin flashback. I was fascinated by space travel. Growing up, I was glued to the TV watching the United States and Russian launches.

Space travel was the big deal then. All this adventure fueled my desire to get in a rocket ship and go myself.

The encyclopedia, the lure of space travel, and the Tintin adventures opened up all the things I wanted to accomplish. I sat down and wrote my highest aspirations in life.

Writing the Script of My Life

I drafted my own screenplay of goals. I was the actor, the producer, and the director. Here I am as an eight-year-old, with my list of ten life goals. Pretty ambitious. Dreaming and thinking big. That list has fueled my life. Since writing down that list at age eight, I've accomplished almost everything on the list. I have two major goals remaining: rocketing to a space station orbiting 250 miles above the Earth and walking on the moon. Even those goals are within my reach.

My Adventures

I became the first flight-qualified, certified civilian astronaut from Australia, and was a backup astronaut for the TMA 13 NASA/Russian space mission. I remain in mission allocation status for a future space flight to the International Space Station.

181

For a few years, I lived in Moscow and graduated from the Yuri Gagarin Cosmonaut Training Center in Star City. During the Communist era, Soviet cosmonauts were quietly chosen, groomed, and trained behind a veil of secrecy.

My life has been filled with extreme adventures. I have visited over 152 countries. I have trekked with the Tuareg Bedouins across the Sahara Desert. I broke the sound barrier in a modified Russian MIG 25 supersonic interceptor jet traveling at almost Mach 3.2 (2,170 mph, 3,470 kmh) and viewed the curvature of the earth. My rock band performed and toured with big names like Bon Jovi and Deep Purple. I dived down five miles deep in a pressurized biosphere to have lunch on the bow of the shipwreck RMS Titanic in the North Atlantic Ocean.

I have climbed the highest peaks of five continents, including the mighty Mt. Aconcagua in the Andes. I have two more peaks to summit on my attempt to become one of a handful of climbers in history who have climbed the Seven Summits—the highest mountains of all seven of the world's continents. I did a Navy Seals HALO skydive jump with oxygen, above the summit of Mt. Everest in Nepal at over 30,000 feet, on my most recent birthday. I have rappelled into the heart of the most active volcanoes in the world. I have storm-chased tornadoes in the Midwest and hurricanes across the Atlantic Ocean.

I even negotiated with the former deposed dictator of Egypt to spend a night in the nearly 5,000-year-old Cheops Pyramid in Giza, Egypt. I spent the night alone in the King's Chamber of the pyramid and slept in the sarcophagus in total darkness—the very same sarcophagus that Napoleon Bonaparte, Alexander the Great, Herodotus, Sir Isaac Newton, and other giants of history had slept in. Media outlets dubbed me the "Thrillionaire."

"Don't be an extra in your own movie"
—Bob Proctor

My Worldwide Business

During the last two decades, my companies have impacted more than one million people in fifty-seven countries. I deliver keynote speeches and facilitate entrepreneurial training courses around the world. I even get the opportunity to speak in remote locations most foreigners would simply never visit. Just recently, I spoke in the communist "hermit kingdom" of North Korea and taught geography to a classroom of teenagers about to graduate. I have conducted an entrepreneurial mastermind seminar to more than 750 investors and business owners in Tehran, Iran.

Do not go where the path may lead, go instead where there is no path and leave a trail.

—Ralph Waldo Emerson

It's Time to Live Your Dreams

My adventurous life did not happen because I was born into wealth. Lacking a wealthy friend such as Tintin's Captain Haddock, I realized that if I wanted to become an adventurer like Tintin, I would need to develop multiple pillars of

183

income in order to afford such a lifestyle. I wasn't born rich—but I was born rich in human potential. My life by design was never coincidental or lucky. I have merely acted out the script I created for my life—a screenplay I wrote as a young child. My manifested reality was the result of every decision made in my life. I did have medical issues earlier in my childhood, but I refused to be held captive by them. I was forced to clear any obstacles that threatened to obstruct my path of self-discovery.

I'm no more special than anyone else. I've simply set my sights on big goals and have never stopped working to achieve them. There's nothing stopping you from doing the same. You may not care about traveling or anything else I've done. I don't share my life experiences with you because I think you should care about anything I've accomplished, but rather to simply inspire you to live your own version of the ideal life.

There is no shortage of adventures to live and thrills to be experienced. You may want to live on the beach and surf every day. Perhaps you want to go on an epic RV trip. Your dream could be to do frequent humanitarian trips to developing countries. Maybe you just want to spend more time with your family or simply have the leisure time to read more.

Whatever it is for you, go after it. Don't let anyone tell you it's impossible; don't let anything stop you. Life is the greatest show on earth. Ensure you have front-row seats. You have an abundance of opportunities that people in the past could not even have dreamed of. Eliminate all excuses from your mind and vocabulary. Cut off the pessimists and haters in your life. Surround yourself with inspirational people, and immerse yourself in inspirational material. Do whatever it takes to escape the trap of the ordinary. Because I can promise you this:

It is so worth it.

"Start by doing what's necessary; then do what's possible; and suddenly you are doing the impossible"

—St. Francis of Assisi

Biography

Nik Halik, The Thrillionaire® Entrepreneurial Alchemist, Civilian Astronaut, Extreme Adventurer, Keynote Speaker is the founder and chief executive officer of Financial Freedom Institute, Lifestyle Revolution, and 5 Day Weekend®. He became a multimillionaire and amassed great wealth through investments in property, business, and the financial markets. Nik's group of companies have financially educated and life coached more than 1 million clients in 57 countries. Nik generates passive income, building recurring subscription businesses, investing in tech startups, and multi-family apartment complexes. He is currently an angel investor and strategic adviser for several tech start-ups in the United States.

Halik has traveled to more than 150 countries, dived to the wreck of RMS Titanic to have lunch on the bow, been active as a mountaineer on some of the world's highest peaks, performed a high-altitude low-opening (HALO) skydive above the summit of Mt. Everest in the Himalayas, climbed into the crater of an exploding erupting volcano (1,700 degrees F) for an overnight sleepover, and just recently, entered North Korea to expose a sweatshop factory operating illegally for an American conglomerate.

He was the back-up astronaut for the NASA / Russian Soyuz TMA-13 flight to the International Space Station in 2008. He remains in mission allocation status for a future flight to Earth's only manned outpost in orbit—the International Space Station with Russia.

Contact Information:

www.FollowNik.com

CHAPTER NINETEEN

Finding 'Papa'

Jayln Nicola

When I was a child, I always dreamed about joining the military. My friends were dreaming about becoming doctors and lawyers, and I knew those careers just were not for me.

I was eighteen when I first tried to enlist in the military. Though my first choice was the Navy, enlisting didn't work out, so I decided to try the Air Force. When I walked into the recruiting office in Bayshore, the airman behind the desk told me I needed to be smart to join the Air Force.

"Well, I guess all those times I was told that I'd never amount to anything and I'd never go anywhere were completely true," I said to myself and I turned to walk out of the office.

Before I got to the door, something told me to stop and walk to the other side of the office, the Army side, where there were more soldiers. That's where I met Army Sergeant First Class (SFC) Phelps, and I will never forget him. We went through some good times and some trying times together.

My mother was completely against me joining the Armed Forces. Though she told me the military was for boys, not girls,

I decided to enlist anyway.

On the morning of September 11, 2001, I was driving into New York City, and I saw a plane flying very low. Once I arrived at Fort Hamilton in Brooklyn, I was sent underground, and I had no idea what was going on. All I remember was the chaos and people saying, "Oh, my God! They hit us in our backyard."

After seeing the devastation across the river, I knew I was making the right decision. I spoke to the recruiter and signed up that same day, September 11. Sergeant Phelps asked me, "So, you did it, huh?"

"Yes, but they didn't have the job I wanted, so they gave me another one."

"Oh yeah? What did you get?"

"I got 92G."

He looked at me and said with a crazy grin, "Uhm, do you know what that is?"

"Nope, but it sounds cool."

"Well, I'm sorry to break the news to you, troop, but you will be a cook."

I looked at him and said a few choice words. I had wanted to be a mechanic. "Well, how bad can it really be? At least I'll finally be getting out of New York," I said.

I went home and did not say anything about what I had done. About a week before I was supposed to ship out, I told my mom and family I had enlisted. I knew if I had told them earlier, they would figure out a way to talk me out of what I was meant to do.

On September 24, 2001, I took a Greyhound bus to Fort Jackson, South Carolina, for basic training. The moment we arrived, the drill instructors came on the bus and told us to put our heads down, then they started yelling at us to get off the bus. We grabbed our bags and that is when I started to learn what it was to be alone.

They took everything we owned away from us. We could not move without them saying so. We could not speak without asking for permission. Our "Hell Week" began and it really was mentally and physically stressful. This was the first time I was away from my family, and I had a hard time with the physical training, too—I wasn't in good shape.

After graduating from basic training, I went to Advanced Individual Training at Fort Lee, Virginia, to learn how to be a food service specialist. Once I completed all my training, I was assigned to my duty station in Fort Campbell, Kentucky.

"Oh, my God!" I said to myself after arriving. It was such a different place. I had never seen a horse and carriage as a mode of transportation. I was terrified. I called my girlfriend, Raquel, and told her I was completely homesick. I had gone from one place to another with only a two-week stay at home. I had four years to go without my family.

"Baby," Raquel told me, "Whatever you do, and wherever you are, picture me by your side and you will never be alone."

So, that is what I did, and yes, it worked.

The next day, I woke up and had to repack because my unit was in the field training and I needed to join them. I threw my bags into the HMMWV (High-Mobility Multipurpose Wheeled Vehicle) and off I went. Here is where I needed to put all my previous training into play. During my first encounter with my Section Sergeant, he sent me out to find a Form for him.

"Private, I need you to go to the Platoon Sergeant and ask for a *DA Form TR Double E*," he said.

I had no idea what he wanted.

"Roger, Sergeant," I responded and off I went.

I followed my orders and went to the Platoon Sergeant and requested *DA Form TR Double E*.

"I actually don't have any of those here. However, if you go to the First Sergeant, he will give you that particular Form," he responded.

So, off I went to the first sergeant.

"Excuse me, First Sergeant? My Section Sergeant needs a *DA Form TR Double E*. I've gone to the Platoon Sergeant as well and he didn't have any, so I was told to come and see you. Do you have this Form? We need it for the dining facility."

And of course, he did not have it either.

The First Sergeant sent me to the Commander.

Now, here is the thing. As I was going from person to person, I had absolutely no idea they were all following me.

When I arrived at the Commander's office, I made the same request.

"Excuse me, sir, I was told to come and see you by the First Sergeant. I need to get a *DA Form TR Double E* and no one seems to have it," I said. "We need it for the dining facility."

The Commander looked at me and then looked in the opposite direction.

"Soldier what Form is it that you need?" he asked.

"Sir, I believe it's called a *DA Form TR Double E*," I replied.

"Do me a favor, Soldier, and write it down for me," the Commander instructed.

I wrote it out "T-R-E-E."

This entire time I had been "in the woods looking for trees." Once I figured it out, I felt like such a fool. I was embarrassed and I could not understand why these people, whom I had never met before, would do such a thing.

When I got back to my unit, everyone was laughing.

"Listen. We are all family here," the Sergeant told me. "I wanted to break the ice because you looked so tense. Please don't take that personally."

After that, I felt as if I *was* one of them. That was a good day.

We stayed in the field for two weeks. I moved around a lot within the different units at Fort Campbell. I was moved to an infantry unit where I met my dear friend, Specialist Gil Mercado. It was the first time I had to deal with infantrymen, with front-line men, which is a different experience for sure. I had some choice words for some of them.

Specialist Mercado and I worked together until we deployed to Iraq in February 2003. I remember one day we sat down together to eat lunch. He grabbed a bowl and went to the salad bar to get his salad, and—as always—his three chicken wings and some tomato soup.

"Gil," I asked him. "What are you eating?"

"Don't knock it until you try it," he replied.

It was tomato soup with jalapenos, shredded mozzarella cheese, and chow mein noodles. Let me tell you, from that day on, I ate tomato soup just like that because it was tremendous. We were talking about the deployment and he told me he knew he needed to go, however he did not want to go.

I will be honest: I did not want to go either, but we both had known since we enlisted that this day might come. I remember looking at his face and on his left cheek, he had a small scratch. I asked him where he got it from. He told me it was from his baby daughter, his little princess. They had been playing around and her nails were not trimmed, and she cut him. We laughed and went back into the office.

That was the last time we spoke.

SPC Mercado was deployed before me. I remember the cold

blistering nights we had getting ready for the move overseas. Once we arrived in country, we were sent to different locations. We drove through the country stopping in different areas to rest. One night, we were told there had been a few casualties and one of them was a cook. We had absolutely no idea who it could have been and received conflicting bits and pieces of information.

SSG Williams said she would find out and came back at 2030 hours.

"Nic, it was him," she told me.

"Who?"

"Merc," she replied.

My heart dropped. I could not breathe; I could not cry. I just sat there.

"Nic, are you OK?" SSG Williams asked me.

"I'm fine," I said and left the building.

The truth is I wasn't fine. Mercado and I told each other we would see each other once we got back. I walked back to my tent all alone. I chose to be alone, even though we were supposed to walk with a battle buddy.

I really didn't care what happened to me after that, and I fell into a deep depression. I could not eat or sleep, and I walked everywhere alone and sat outside my tent by myself. Others would pass me by, never asking what happened or even if I was okay. When I called home for the first time, my family said, "Well, you know everyone must die sometime."

That was not something I wanted to hear at that moment.

After the call, I walked into an open area and found a secret door that led to ammunition stockpiles. All I wanted was for the ammunition to go off while I was in the storage facility, but it did not. I was never really myself after that incident. I thought about killing myself with a machine gun, but for some reason I didn't follow through. However, I did become very reckless and started volunteering for dangerous missions.

Once my tour was over, I went back to the dining facility where Mercado and I met, and I sat at our table. I could not hold back anymore, and I broke down.

I have never eaten tomato soup again.

After I left active duty, I joined the National Guard in New York State full time. I've moved up in the ranks, and I'm now an E7, overseeing our dining facility and inspecting facilities at other bases.

After I joined the Guard, depression and thoughts of suicide began taking a toll on my life. I thought about suicide every day. It felt as if everywhere I went, there was some negative thing said about me or done to me. I was not the only one facing depression issues. Some of my soldiers also were facing suicidal thoughts and depression.

I told my soldiers they could always come to me, no matter what problem they faced, so it was hard for me to send them away. One of my soldiers called me at around 0030 hours and when I picked up the phone and asked who it was, I could hear him crying.

"What is wrong?" I asked.

"I've tried to call other people, but no one answered the phone. You were my last call."

He was sobbing as we spoke for hours on the phone. As I listened to him, I realized I was truly on the ledge with him.

"Thank you, Sergeant, for answering the phone and just listening to me," he told me.

"I'm here for you no matter what. Call me at any time."

When I got off the phone, I realized I had talked someone

off a ledge and immediately began to doubt myself.

"Who the heck do I think I am to give him advice when I was out there standing on the same ledge?" I said to myself.

When I saw him again, he was smiling and had started to receive the help he truly needed. That same month, other soldiers came to me with the same suicidal thoughts I had. With a growing number of soldiers depending on me for help, I knew I had to get myself together, and soon.

My life became even more complicated and stressful when I began my transition from a woman to a man. I knew that the hormones I was taking would make me more depressed and emotional as I went through male puberty. I knew I needed to work on my state of mind.

I started listening to Lesley Brown, Lisa Nichols, and a few other motivational speakers while I was working out in the morning. I stumbled across Nichols by accident and the first time I heard her, I cried. Nichols words made me stop being who I was and made me the person I wanted to be. The one thing they all had in common was that they all spoke of "God."

I was an atheist before I started this mental and physical transformation. I was never able to speak with someone because I was always afraid of losing my job because I was suicidal. I would hear all the motivational speakers and they would say, "Let go and let God." I never knew what that meant until I started this process of change. I would ask for peace in my life all the time.

I could be in a room with the lights off, no television, no radio, no anything, and my head would be filled with noise. Once I started the process, I started letting go and putting everything into the hands of Papa (the name I use for God). I slowly started coming out of the darkness that I was in. I hung affirmations all around my house, including on my workout equipment. Every morning, I would get up and thank Papa for waking me up. I would then look at myself in the mirror and tell myself I was worth it. I could make it out there and whatever I put my mind to doing, I could accomplish. I did it every day.

One evening, my wife and I were discussing something that normally would have upset me. That was the first time I felt complete peace in my life. As I rested on my bed and looked at the wall where my affirmations were visible, I started crying. For the first time in my life, I heard no noise in my head. I felt peace from the bottom of my soul. I knew Papa was with me.

Wherever I go now, I talk about Papa. I will never leave his side and he will never leave mine. I have promised Papa that I will tell people my story to help those who are feeling what I felt.

Now I'm in my second year of male puberty, and I look forward to surgery at the end of 2019. I do not care what others say about me. I want my message to touch millions of people across the globe, and I believe that is my sole purpose in life.

So, I say *thank you*, Papa, I am glad I found you, and thank you again for never leaving my side.

Biography

Jayln was born on Long Island, New York, as Jennifer Nicola. He studied computer engineering and networking at Briarcliffe College before enlisting in the U.S. Army on 9/11. During his career in the military, he has mentored more than three hundred soldiers. Currently an E7, he has four years to go before retiring from the New York National Guard.

He studied business administration at Colorado Technical University's online program and plans to become a successful entrepreneur. He is married to Raquel Rodriguez, and they have two sons and two daughters.

Contact Information:

jnicola1976@gmail.com
Instagram: Jayln Rivera
Facebook: Jayln Rivera

CHAPTER TWENTY

One Day Can Change Your Life

Jonathan Long

One day changed my entire life.

I remember it like it was yesterday: April 5, 2010. It was a day of excitement—both the Opening Day for Major League Baseball and the NCAA National Championship basketball game.

I was eager to go to my first baseball Opening Day event. My friends and I began tailgating around 11 a.m. at the Coors Light Tailgate Party Tent. I was overjoyed because of the pleasant time I was having with the people closest to me.

The atmosphere was like none other I had felt up until that point in my life. Live music blasting, ice cold beer, bright sunshine beaming down on us. Not too hot, not too cold, just right. We continued our tailgating up until the game started and then chugged our drinks so we could head inside for the opening pitch.

We walked into Globe Life Park, and as soon as we stepped in, you could feel an atmosphere of excitement. Lots of smiles, lots of laughter, and great vibes all around me. The

Texas Rangers were opening their season against the Toronto Blue Jays. We went back and forth between our seats to watch the game, the bar for drinks, and the food shops. (I just had to get myself one of those delicious turkey legs.) It took me three innings of searching to find the right spot, but I finally found it.

As I approached the counter to order, my salivary glands were watering just thinking about how good this was going to be. After I was served my order, I immediately bit into my turkey leg and it was like an explosion of indescribably amazing flavor in my mouth. It was well worth the wait. After eating, we went back to one of the bars in the ballpark for another round of drinks, then we went back to our seats and finished watching the game.

It was a close game. After the seventh inning, the score was tied 3-3. In the eighth inning, the Blue Jays pulled ahead by one. Heading into the ninth inning, everyone in the ballpark was on edge. The Jays did not score in their half of the inning, and now it was our turn. After just a few at bats, we scored the tying run. Then just a few batting attempts later, we scored on a walk-off run to win the game with a final score of 5-4.

It was a wonderful day: The Rangers came back and won and I was feeling good from the positive vibes in the stadium. The drinks helped, and my stomach was full of food, and the day was not over yet.

After the game, I found myself with my friends at a local bar, watching the NCAA Championship game, Duke vs Butler. It was a nail-biter that came down to the last shot. Duke was up 61-59 with just two seconds left. Butler inbounded the ball to half court to Gordon Haywood, who turned and put up the shot from around the half-court line. It seemed like the ball was in the air for an eternity as it traveled to the basket. It almost seemed like it was going to go in the basket. The ball hit the inside of the rim and rattled its way out. My team had won the National Championship!

I had stopped drinking after the baseball game and had just one shot to celebrate Duke's championship. My night was complete—at least I thought it was.

After partying for ten-plus hours, I was exhausted and ready to get some rest. I made the poor decision to drive myself home. On the way, I saw the worst thing imaginable: the red and blue lights of a police vehicle driving directly behind me, signaling me to pull over.

As I pulled over, so many thoughts were running through my mind. *What was I doing wrong? Stay calm; you've been through this before. I stopped drinking some time ago so he should not smell alcohol. Just remain calm, Jon.*

The officer stepped out of his vehicle and walked up to mine. He asked me for my license and registration, and I handed it over.

"I received a call that this vehicle has been swerving on the interstate," the officer said to me. "Have you been drinking?"

"Yes, officer, I did have some drinks today," I responded truthfully.

The officer had me step out of the vehicle to perform a field sobriety test, and surprisingly, I passed it.

But then his supervisor arrived on the scene, and the officer who had pulled me over told me quietly, "It's out of my hands now."

The supervisor insisted on performing another field sobriety test. I thought I did as well as before, but he told me I failed and would be arrested on a charge of Driving While Intoxicated

(DWI). The supervisor told me to turn around and place my hands behind my back. Once I was handcuffed and given my Miranda rights, he walked me to the squad car and drove me in to the station.

At the police station, he took my official Blood-Alcohol Content (BAC) level. It was over the legal limit, so I was booked on the DWI charge. Seventeen hours later, I was able to bail myself out. That was just the beginning of what seemed like a never-ending process with the courts. After about five months, I owned up completely and told my lawyer I just wanted it to be over. So, in August, I was sentenced to serve two years' probation and perform 30 hours of community service. I also was required to have an Interlock system installed in my car at my own expense. The device would make it impossible for me to operate my vehicle if I had consumed any alcohol.

Receiving my DWI was an eye-opening experience. It made me realize I could not continue living a life of partying and self-destruction. I needed to change. I just was not sure how to go about it. I did everything required by the judicial system, and I was so, *so* lucky: just two years of probation.

Now it was time for a big change in my life.

In the beginning of my new journey, it was difficult for me to hang out with my friends because all they wanted to do was drink. Legally, I could not do that anymore. I also knew I had been out of control, so it was time to stop anyway.

It took me a while, but I finally realized two things:

My friends needed to change, or,

I needed to change my friends.

That was hardest part of the journey for me. I had been enjoying life. For the first time, I was popular and having the time of my life. I had been feeling a high like I never felt before, because I had never before been considered popular. I did not want to lose the feeling.

While serving out my probation, I realized I wanted and needed more out of life. My dilemma was I didn't know how to accomplish it. As I continued my journey, I realized that if I wanted my life to change, I needed to first change myself.

Once I turned on that switch, magical things started occurring. I stopped blaming other people for what happened to me and I took ownership of my own life. And I realized everything that happens to you has a reason behind it.

Taking ownership of my life and problems caused me to look at things completely differently. I finally understood *I* was in complete control of my life and whether it was going to be good or bad rested squarely on my shoulders.

It is amazing how once you make a decision, everything starts to align. One night, I went to a social mixer and met someone named Ed Blunt. I did not realize that he was an entrepreneur, international speaker, trainer, and author. I definitely did not know at the time that he would alter the course of my life completely and forever. His energy was different from anyone I had ever met. I could feel that Mr. Blunt was different from most people. When he spoke, I became filled with life and positivity and it was uplifting.

As the night went on, I kept thinking to myself how amazing life could be if I could start to dream again. From that day forward, I created a new belief system. I began to share this new vision with my friends but they either did not see it or flat-out could not agree with my outlook on a new life. I decided it didn't matter as much as it would have earlier in my life. I knew this vision was given to me and only me. I began to realize that few people would understand, and I was willing to accept that.

In the beginning of my change, I lost people I thought were my friends. Now I realized they were just associates—people I hung out with because we had common ground.

As I started losing my existing friends, I started gaining new friends who were aligned with my new outlook on life. As I wanted more and needed more, I continued to exchange old friends for new friends who shared similar beliefs.

I started to expand my thinking. My head was filled with thoughts of positivity, goal setting, and reading and educating myself in the direction I desired to go. I focused more on personal development because I realized I had to become a better person. Once I became a better person, naturally I would become better in other aspects of life. So, I started reading books. Books on leadership, relationships, communication, thinking bigger, and being more efficient. In addition, I listened to audio recordings to further expose myself to new ways of thinking while commuting to and from work.

I often would listen to motivational speakers such as Johnny Wimbrey, Trent Shelton, Les Brown, Eric Thomas, Jim Rohn, Earl Nightingale, and the list goes on. I attended different seminars. I did everything I could to better myself. Until then, I never realized how many people wanted more out of life, just as I now did. It was a blessing to meet people who push you in the right direction—toward greatness. To be great, I realized I needed to be a student of the game.

If anyone were to ask me if I am successful, I would say, "Yes. I am successful because I have grown as a person. I communicate more efficiently and because of that, my relationship with people is better. I understand them better and I am more open to listening to their points of view."

And there is a lot more depth to my success as well, as I've learned a great deal about the power of thinking. Our dreams and thoughts take shape as a form of reality and what we focus on expands. As I've grown into leadership, I've realized one of the more important aspects is becoming the leader with dreams whom everyone wants to follow. I have been and am continuing to be mentored by leaders with powerful dreams, and I respect and emulate them.

As time passes and I connect with others, I pay the mentorship forward the way it was taught to me. I am currently working at Texas Live in Arlington, Texas, but I also work on my own personal business in the travel industry while I transition from employee to entrepreneur. I would love to tell you the rest of my story, but much like yours, my story is still being written.

I plan for the future, yet still live and cherish the precious moments in the now, just taking it one day at a time.

Biography

Jonathan Long wakes up every day hoping to inspire at least one person. He was born on November 21, 1985, in El Paso, Texas to Kevin and Fran Long. He graduated from South Hills High School in South Fort Worth, Texas, and then attended Tarrant County College for Communication Broadcasting in an effort to fulfill a childhood dream of becoming a disc jockey before electing to pursue another profession in the service industry. Long began his career in bartending because after being shy growing up, he developed a love for being around and interacting with people.

Jonathan is single and has no children.

He is currently transitioning from the service industry to entrepreneurship. While building his business is important and he has many goals in doing so, his ultimate goal in life is to serve, lead, and inspire others to reach and maximize their fullest potential as a person and in their careers. Jonathan plans to become a mentor to more people as his skills continue to develop.

One of the ways he improves his leadership skills and moves toward his goals is by speaking life and positivity into others.

Contact Information:

Email: JonathanTLong2004@gmail.com
Facebook: Jonathan Long
Instagram: Jonathan_T_Long

CHAPTER TWENTY-ONE

Flex On Your World And Succeed In It

LaRita Phelps

As I predicted when I started on this writing journey, my three children and I are now in a *Women in Need* homeless shelter for families. We are two to three hours—a city bus ride, a ferry ride, a train ride, and then another city bus ride—away from Staten Island, which we previously called home. I never in a million years would have imagined that we would actually end up in a shelter, and must stay for at least three months to even begin to get the help we need to acquire our own place to call *home*.

At the Women in Need shelter, we are completely isolated from our friends and family because there's a "no visitor" rule. So, when we are not in school, at work, or at appointments, we are cooped up in this bedroom/kitchenette/dining room/ bathroom unit with two sets of bunk beds, a five-drawer metal cabinet (that we do not trust enough to put our clothes in), an in-counter two-burner hotplate, a small table with two chairs for four people. I say *unit* because the case managers have made it very clear what it is not.

It is definitely not *home*. We won't even say, "We are going *home*" or "Are you on your way *home?*" This place just isn't *home* to us. It is just *here* or *there*. It is our *temporary unit* until we become independent again.

When I was told we'd have to leave the bedroom loaned to us by a close family friend, I was told by another that going into a shelter would be what's *best* for us. Psychologically and emotionally, it has not been anything close to being the best thing. Going into a shelter took away an invisible visible piece of us, individually as well as collectively. The shelter took away our independence.

Since moving to our current residence right around the corner from LaGuardia Airport, my eldest daughter has had multiple anxiety attacks and has since been diagnosed with severe anxiety and Post Traumatic Stress Disorder (PTSD). My daughter's problems were probably triggered when I threw her father out of the house after more than 16 years. I needed my children to know they should never accept being mistreated nor should they mistreat anyone else. They needed to know their self-worth was more valuable than the most exotic of jewels.

My assessment by social workers concluded that my own anxiety, PTSD (from being emotionally, physically, and sexually abused for years by my stepfather), and depression have gotten worse since being in the shelter. The only good thing that has come from us being here so far is that we will all receive the help we so desperately need.

By being in this place, with no real choice, we had to temporarily give up our two rescued one-year-old kittens. They have been with us since they were each only a few weeks old. We are the only family they had ever known or remembered, other than each other. They were traumatized because we had to leave them with the only person I could think of who would be willing to take them temporarily, someone they had never laid eyes on before.

The kittens' foster mom has a busy work schedule and we are only able to visit them once a week. Sunday after church. We are traumatized because we just learned that when we leave, the more social kitten, Domino, follows us to the door and cries for us. The younger kitten, Fluffy, constantly stays hidden and only emerges when there are no humans in the house or when we visit and call her out. Even then, I'm the only one for whom she completely emerges. This brought my eldest to tears and I broke down at a Social Security preliminary evaluation, which is still pending.

You might ask why do I need Social Security when I'm only 40 years old. Four years ago, I was injured at work. Who'd have thought a slip and fall on an icy ramp would result in my losing my health, my car, my well-paid job, our apartment, and nearly my sanity? I was already in a fragile state emotionally because of my fear of traveling alone via public transportation, which developed after my car was repossessed after weeks of my trying to hide it. The day came when I went to get in the car and it was gone. The bank had found what we were trying our best to hide.

With all that had happened and was happening, I became overwhelmingly afraid of falling. I tend to lose my balance at random moments and just fall. Falling again could cause more harm to my already permanently injured back. I had already developed saddle paresthesia—numbness and tingling from the waist down, starting in my groin area. I had already walked my eldest daughter into her high school graduation using a walker. I had already gained a lack of being able to stand, sit or walk for very long without my hands and feet going numb with my back screaming out in pain, joining in the song of pain my knee also screamed.

Going through these traumatic events doesn't compare to what I've managed to keep my children in the know about while being nothing but humble, grateful, positive thinking/speaking, and prayed up. I did this while always claiming *nothing* but the best is yet to come for *all* of us.

I am honestly amazed at the way my youngest saw nothing but the good things and never once got sad about our circumstances while she still fully grasped where we were living. She was super excited about being on the top bunk with her big sister on the bottom bunk. She was super excited to get her meager Christmas gifts courtesy of the shelter's staff. She was super excited to be goofy with us.

Then I realized she's still happy and smiling because we are all together.

My youngest, a 10-year-old Mini Me, simply displayed all that I have ever taught her, her 16-year-old brother, and 21-year-old sister before her—to see the *best* in any situation, not the worst, and to speak of what you want while saying *when* rather than *if*.

But then came the day when we discovered that same optimistic beautiful 10-year-old girl was harming herself because that was the only way she could find to handle all that she was feeling inside and holding onto. She hurt herself, while always checking on us, making sure we were coping and always asking, "Are you okay?" We never once realized she was hurting *so* much that she could only use the dividing of her skin with a kitchen utensil to relieve that pain, pressure, and hurt.

It completely took us off guard, but it let me know that we needed to be there for each other more than ever and could not let life in the shelter eat us alive, kill our spirits, or kill us literally. Our hard times, down times, and rock bottom times cannot steal our happiness. As my grandparents always said, "The devil is a lie!"

And so, we reinforced our being together, physically able to open our eyes, take a breath, and move, even if painfully, when there are some who are worse off than we are at our lowest. We had only two weeks' worth of clothing, only two pairs of shoes, and only two bags each of personal items. Some of the things in those bags contained things we all shared, such as hair care and body hygiene products.

My breakthrough came when I realized I had forgotten the most important lesson I've ever taught my children:

"Always see and speak positivity over your lives and situations and circumstances."

How could I let my current situation dictate what my future would be? Our *now* only prepares us for our *tomorrow*, never being dictated by, but born out of our yesterday.

How could I not speak my success into existence? My success had already been written from the time I was formed in my mother's womb. God spoke a storm over my life while also speaking into existence beautiful things to be formed from that storm.

Why would I do such a thing to myself and let my children see me do the exact opposite of what I've always taught and told them to do? Never accept negativity—even if it is staring you down while beating you down. And so, we claim nothing but victory over our lives together and individually.

The situation we are in will not determine where we will be a year from now or a decade from now. Our commute back to our lives is a lot longer, but we smile and laugh about it while observing our physical surroundings are those that many envy. Our location is one that most never have the privilege to experience—the Big Apple. New York City. We still return to Staten Island from Flushing, Queens, to worship, to work, to go to school, to go to doctor appointments, and to visit our family and friends.

The situation we are in isn't our final revelation, not after all the hell we've—I've—been through. I refuse to allow this to break me and turn me into a victim instead of a victor and survivor, and I'll be damned if I'll let it victimize my children, either.

I survived being sexually abused for more than a decade of my youth. I have survived my father not being there until I became a mother myself, feeling unloved, unwanted, and unprotected most of my life. I have survived having little to eat but making meals from what was in the cabinets and fridge.

I survived a drug-addicted stepfather threatening to kill my mother while he beat the spirit out of her. I survived watching my stepfather's drug habits and extramarital escapades with prostitutes, kill my mother—figuratively and literally. I survived losing my mother after watching her deteriorate from complications from one of the scariest diseases ever to exist: Human Immunodeficiency Virus/Acquired Immunodeficiency Syndrome. H.I.V. / A.I.D.S. Before she died, she had me tested, after learning that her biggest fear was my reality. I was being sexually abused by the same man who gave HIV to her. By God's grace and mercy, I have always tested negative. I have survived the fear of having that as well as the fear of anyone ever finding this out and treating me...us..."differently."

I survived an emotionally abusive relationship that, in the beginning, became a damaging physically violent one (often times initiated by my frustrations of his mistreatment of our relationship...even after having our first, second, third, fourth and fifth child), allowing him to convince me that no one would ever want me again. Though we had five children, only three were born into this world. Two of them were aborted and I survived being forced to go through that trauma without their father because he believed they were fathered by another man, which is not true. Because abortion is something I don't truly believe in, except in cases of rape or incest, the two I had still haunt me. When it was time for me to have mine and commit my personal suicide/murder, I saw my second baby, whom I named Chance, on the sonogram screen while with my fourth baby, whom I named Serenity, kicked as she was suffering in my womb from the first phase of my two phase abortion. I am *still* recovering from what I had to do.

I survived my maternal grandmother passing away less than two years after leaving New York, feeling helpless while she was being mistreated because she told me she was "okay," though I later learned she truly wasn't.

I survived being harassed by the New York City Housing Authority's building manager and eventually being physically and embarrassingly, evicted from our home. I spent the night in a car while my two oldest children slept on our terrace in the cold with my younger brother watching them and our stuff to ensure no one stole anything while we scrambled to rent another moving van. It was actually the *second* moving van because the first one we had was towed away by the moving company with our personal items still in it—while I was on the phone with the rental company trying to figure out how to replace the key we misplaced. The key to the van had been lost while we were trying to get our stuff out of the apartment as the marshals packed up our lives into brown boxes.

The marshals weren't concerned with whether or not all our belongings made it into those boxes and my children wound up leaving and losing so many of their belongings—some of which were sentimental and cannot be replaced. But we were together and we had our health, heading into a situation that was only temporary, leading up to our second eviction only eight months later.

I survived all the years of never feeling good enough, believing that giving "good" sex to the male I was dealing with made me good enough. I survived doing what I believed I needed to do to get my children what they needed when I involuntarily became a single parent. I survived multiple suicide attempts and self-mutilations, never understanding why—until now.

My role is to be the survivor and help other victims and survivors to get to their redemption song, showing them that what hasn't killed them may bend them but will never break them. I will show them that while they are going through their current personal hell, it only dents their armor and prepares them for the multiple stories of their lives—their success story, their survival story, and the story of their breakthrough to a better life. My role is to show them that if *I* can survive and become somebody, so can they.

Though I always felt unworthy or not good enough, my oldest daughter and I became entrepreneurs with an amazing worldwide company. She reminded me daily that what I felt about myself was a lie. Despite coming from a legacy of poverty, we are now able to travel the world together or with our friends (some of whom became more like family than my actual family) or alone enjoying folks in the destination once we got there, while creating a financial legacy, and leaving my great-grandchildren residual income rather than residual bills.

I have learned that *all* of my traumas were only meant to strengthen my muscles as I flex at all the bullsh*t being slung my way.

I was weeping while being beaten. I flex at it now.

I was being sexually abused and I hid. I show off and flex at it now.

I was told I was garbage and believed it *then*. *Now,* I flex at it like I am in a competition for flexing.

I used my body to take care of my babies. I still use my body—to flex at that shame as I get up and get to work on my success.

Get up and flex on that weak hell in your life because it is nothing to cringe from, hide from, or shrink from.

My journey may be different from any other person's journey, but who can say any of us won't become the survivor who saves another's life just by telling their truth? Only God can make that call. God made me the student of a coach, teaching and training me for my survival, without telling me that my beat-ups were my come-ups.

I am, have *always* been, and *will* always be "fearfully and wonderfully made"

. . . just like you are—you who are now reading this.

Now go *flex* on your world and *succeed* in it!

Biography

LaRita Phelps, born in Fort Riley, Kansas on a military base to two active duty Army soldiers, has lived in New York City since she was a toddler.

LaRita is an aspiring Mompreneur with two daughters and one son, all of whom are beautifully blessed and artistically gifted.

As a dedicated mother and strong woman, she sets an example as to how one can overcome life's adversities as a survivor who will Pray Until Something Happens instead of being a victim who gets pushed over the edge.

LaRita has been writing poetry and short stories since childhood as a way to express her feelings and to be heard when she felt no one would listen. At age 17, her poetry blossomed into lyrics sung by others which established her as a lyricist with a membership with B.M.I. and A.S.C.A.P. She has also worked with several producers she met while working at Sam Ash Music as a singer/songwriter.

As an active member of Fellowship Baptist Church since the age of 14, she has held titles on several ministries, is active in various church functions.

Contact Information

Email: lcphelps0478@gmail.com
Facebook: LaRita Phelps
Instagram: @LC_PHELPS
YouTube: youtube.com/unique0478
Twitter: @LaRitaPhelps429

CHAPTER TWENTY-TWO

The "Real" You

Les Brown

Sometimes it's not about changing to become the person you *want* to be; it's about changing to become the person you *need* to be. There is a whole big, expectant world out there waiting on you to do the things you were destined to do – and the only obstacle in the way is YOU. Personal growth can help you conquer that obstacle, but you must first be a willing participant.

Once you have decided that you are that willing participant, follow these four easy stages of increased awareness to help you begin this journey to a "new you." Let's take a quick look at how 1) self-knowledge, 2) self-approval, 3) self-commitment and 4) self-fulfillment intertwine to help you consciously step into greatness.

First of all, in order to see yourself beyond your current circumstances, you must master **self-knowledge**. Simply ask yourself, "What drives me?" And then pause long enough to hear your response. Try to understand what outside forces – positive or negative – are influencing your answer. Many of us suffer from what I call "unconscious incompetence." That means we don't know that we don't know, which leaves the door wide open for others to tell us what we think we need to know. Therefore, before you can fully wake up and change your life, you must understand the frame of reference from which you view the world. Study yourself, study the forces behind your personal history, and study the people in your life. This will help liberate you to grow beyond your imagination.

The second, and perhaps most crucial, stage of personal growth is **self-approval**. Once you begin to know and understand yourself more completely, then you must accept and love yourself. Self-hatred, self-loathing, guilt and long-standing anger only work to block your growth. Don't direct your energy toward this type of self-destruction. Instead, practice self-love and forgiveness and watch how they carry over into your relationships, your work and the world around you, opening up the possibility for others to love you, too. If you need help in boosting your self-approval, try these steps: 1) focus on your gifts, 2) write down at least five things you like about yourself, 3) think about the people who make you feel special, and 4) recall your moments of triumph.

When you are committed to taking life on, life opens up for you. Only then do you become aware of things that you were not aware of before. That is the essence of **self-commitment**. It's like the expanded consciousness that comes whenever I commit to a diet. Suddenly, everywhere I turn, there is FOOD! Or how about when you buy a new car? Suddenly you notice cars exactly like yours, everywhere you go. Well, likewise, when you make a commitment – when your life awareness is expanded – opportunities previously unseen begin to appear, bringing you to a higher level. In this posture, you are running your life, rather than running *from* life.

The fourth stage of self awareness is **self-fulfillment**. Once you have committed to something and achieved it, you then experience a sense of success and empowerment, otherwise known as fulfillment. Your drive for self-fulfillment should be an unending quest; a continual sequence of testing self-knowledge, fortifying self-approval, renewing self-commitment and striving for new levels of self-fulfillment. Once you have accomplished a goal and reached a level of self-fulfillment, it is then time to go back to the first stage in the cycle.

These four stages create synergy for a conscious awareness of your personal growth. But what about learning to deal with all this from a subconscious standpoint? A very interesting book I have read entitled, "A Whole New Mind," by Daniel H. Pink, explains that the key to success today is in the hands of the individual with a whole different kind of thinking than what our informational age has molded us to. The metaphorically "left brain" capacities that fueled that Information Era, are no longer sufficient. Instead, ""right brain" traits of inventiveness, empathy, joyfulness and meaning – increasingly will determine who flourishes and who flounders." (Pink, 2007)

I highly recommend that, in the midst of your busy schedule, if you haven't done so already, pick up this book and engage yourself to a fresh look at what it takes to excel. As I mentioned before, the only real obstacle in your path to personal growth and a fulfilling life is you. If everything around you is changing and growing – then change and grow. Do it today. Remember, we are all counting on you to step into your greatness!

Now even after making all of these changes what would you say if someone walked up to you and asked, "Who are you?" Would you stutter or hesitate before giving some sort of answer? Would you make up something that sounded impressive, but that you know isn't exactly true? Well, to accurately answer the question of who you are, you must first get in touch with the person who lives and breathes on the inside of you.

When you know and understand who you were made to be, you can begin to tap into the innate power of your own uniqueness. That power allows you the freedom to no longer let life hold you back because of nonsense based on what you've done or not done. It gives you the positive energy to move forward in spite of those things.

You are a unique individual. Think about it, out of 400,000,000 sperm, one was spared to allow you to be here today. Then once you got here, you came with total exclusivity! I know for a fact, as a twin myself, how you can look like someone else, even sound like that person, yet when you consider the total you, there is only one. Wow! Just let that thought sink down in you for a moment.

Now, hopefully that helps you to realize that there is a certain quality on the inside of you that was given to you – and only you – in order to make a difference in this world. Whatever that quality is, it was not intended for you to sit on it, or waste it away. Oh no, it was given to you for a purpose! You cannot, however, learn what that purpose is unless you look inside and see what makes your existence so special.

Don't waste time trying to find "you" in other people. When you compare yourself to others, or try to be like them, you deny yourself – and the universe – the opportunity to be blessed by the gifts and talents that were given only to you. You are destined to achieve great things in *your* own special way; not in the same manner as your friends, relatives, co-workers, colleagues or even mentors. Doing so will only leave you unsatisfied. When you are not satisfied, regret creeps in.

If you don't know this already, let me share a little secret with you: In order to live a good life – a life full of purpose and resolve – you must live it with NO REGRETS!

Most people go through their whole life with a long "would've, could've, should've" list. The truth of the matter is, once you've lived through a day, an hour, or a minute, it's done. You cannot go back. So get over it! Go forward! There's so much more for you to accomplish that you don't have time to live in the past trying to fix things.

Keep in mind, though, that living in the past and reflecting on the past are two totally different things. You *can* look back –

and you should – in order to determine what it was about certain experiences that brought you joy and satisfaction, or grief and despair; what caused you to grow and expand your horizons, or left you stagnant and short-sighted.

Although you cannot relive the past, you can learn much about yourself as a result of having lived it. That requires a lot of honesty with yourself, as well as a willingness to do **whatever it takes** to reach your destiny. Of all the things you can acquire in this life, the most valuable has to be the knowledge of what role you are to play on this earth, for the sake of your destiny.

My favorite book says to *"Lean not on your own understanding, but in all your ways, acknowledge Him and He will direct your paths."* In other words, don't rely solely on your own insight regarding what your role is. There's a Creator who made you and knows you better than you know yourself. Therefore, in everything you do, in every direction you take, recognize and consult with that Creator. That's what it means to look on the inside – not at others.

Now, you will have a real answer when someone asks, "Who are you?" You can assure them that, without a shadow of a doubt, you are not here by accident. You can articulate with unwavering conviction what it is you were put on this earth to do. **Learn to do this and watch the real "you" shine through!**

Biography

Les Brown is a top Motivational Speaker, Speech Coach, and Best-Selling Author, loving father and grandfather, whose passion is empowering youth and helping them have a larger vision for their lives.

Les Brown's straight-from-the-heart, high-energy, passionate message motivates and engages all audiences to step into their greatness, providing them with the motivation to take the next step toward living their dream. Les Brown's charisma, warmth and sense of humor have impacted many lives.

Les Brown's life itself is a true testament to the power of positive thinking and the infinite human potential. Leslie C. Brown was born on February 17, 1945, in an abandoned building on a floor in Liberty City, a low-income section of Miami, Florida, and adopted at six weeks of age by Mrs. Mamie Brown, a 38 year old single woman, cafeteria cook and domestic worker, who had very little education or financial means, but a very big heart and the desire to care for Les Brown and his twin brother, Wesley Brown. Les Brown calls himself "Mrs. Mamie Brown's Baby Boy" and claims "All that I am and all that I ever hoped to be, I owe to my mother".

Les Brown's determination and persistence searching for ways to help Mamie Brown overcome poverty and his philosophy "do whatever it takes to achieve success" led him to become a distinguished authority on harnessing human potential and success. Les Brown's passion to learn and his hunger to realize greatness in himself and others helped him to achieve greatness in spite of not having formal education or training beyond high school.

"My mission is to get a message out that will help people become uncomfortable with their mediocrity. A lot of people are content with their discontent. I want to be the catalyst that enables them to see themselves having more and achieving more."

Les moved to Detroit and rented an office with an attorney, where he slept on the floor and welcomed his reality stating that he did not even want a blanket or pallet on the cold, hard floor to keep him motivated to strive. In 1986, Les entered the public speaking arena on a full-time basis and formed his own company, Les Brown Enterprises, Inc..

Les Brown rose from a hip-talking morning DJ to broadcast manager; from community activist to community leader; from political commentator to three-term State legislator in Ohio; and from a banquet and nightclub emcee to premier Keynote Speaker for audiences as big as 80,000 people, including Fortune 500 companies and organizations all over the world.

As a caring and dedicated Speech Coach, Les Brown has coached and trained numerous successful young speakers all over the nation.

Les Brown is also the author of the highly acclaimed and successful books, "Live Your Dreams" and "It's Not Over Until You Win", and former host of The Les Brown Show, a nationally syndicated daily television talk show which focused on solutions and not on problems.

Contact Information:

www.lesbrown.com

 thelesbrown

 @LesBrown77

 @thelesbrown

 LesBrown

 LinkedIn@

www.ingramcontent.com/pod-product-compliance
Lightning Source LLC
Chambersburg PA
CBHW061254110426
42742CB00012BA/1917